06/10
10.95

The **Family Tree Maker** 2010

Little
of Book
Answers

Tips, Tools, and Extras

P9-EBB-423

D0782972

The **Family Tree Maker** 2010

Little
of Book
Answers

Tips, Tools, and Extras

Tana L. Pedersen

⊰| **ancestry**publishing

Library of Congress Cataloging-in-Publication Data

Pedersen, Tana L.
The Family tree maker 2010 little book of answers : tips, tools, and extras / Tana L.
Pedersen.
    p. cm.
Includes index.
ISBN 978-1-59331-331-9 (alk. paper)
1. Family tree maker. 2. Genealogy—Computer programs. 3. Genealogy—Data
processing. I. Title.
CS14.P428 2009
929'.10285—dc22

2009024766

10 9 8 7 6 5 4 3

ISBN-978-1-59331-331-9
Printed in the United States of America.

Contents

Introduction

A few years ago I was entering several new generations into my Family Tree Maker file, and the same names seemed to be appearing over and over again. No surprise really—everyone in that branch of my tree seemed to be named Samuel, Benjamin, or Elizabeth. Then one day as I stared at a list of family names, I had an epiphany. The reason why all those people were so similar was because they *were* the same people. I hadn't recognized it before, but I had two ancestors who were cousins and had married each other. I had faithfully entered the same branch of my family tree, twice.

I suspect that I'm not the only family historian who has dealt with this kind of situation. Whether it's your great-grandfather who appears to have married every young woman in the county or that elusive female you just can't prove is actually related to you, we've all struggled to figure out the best ways to record these types of genealogy puzzles.

And recently, when the state of Utah put thousands of digital images of death records online, I was able to view the causes of death (and contributing health factors) for several of my ancestors and some collateral relatives. When I saw a pattern of coronary heart disease and stroke, I became interested in gathering even more medical information about my relatives and creating a family health history.

When I began writing *The Official Guide to Family Tree Maker 2008*, both of these experiences were in the forefront of my thoughts. Because the official guide covers every available feature in the software, I only have time to discuss the basic use of each component; I don't have much opportunity to discuss the exceptional situations that present themselves in every family. And the idea for this book was born.

While each family tree has its own snags and unique challenges, there are some common dilemmas that most of us face at some time or another as we try to record our ancestors' lives. I have used examples from my own personal research and family tree to guide you through some of these real-life scenarios.

You do not need to be an expert family historian or even an advanced user of Family Tree Maker to take advantage of the explanations in this guide. Step-by-step instructions will walk you through even the most difficult tasks.

In addition, this guide doesn't need to be read from cover to cover. Feel free to jump from topic to topic and look over the subjects that discuss issues that are important to you. I've also included some custom reports that I've found useful either for sharing my finds with other family members or tracking my research so I know where to look next. I hope you'll find them useful too.

If you have difficult situations you've faced in your family history that aren't covered in this guide, or if you have your own tips on how best to correct these situations, I'd love to hear from you. I can be contacted at tpedersen@ancestry.com. A special thanks to all the readers who e-mailed me after the last two editions with questions, comments, and conundrums. I have included several topics based on your feedback that I hope will help users everywhere.

Best of luck with your family history search.

Address Report

Every year when my Reed family holds its annual reunion, someone has to gather the addresses of every family member in order to send out instructions, assignments, and directions to the location. I discovered that an easy way to gather this information is by putting each family's address (or e-mail address) in Family Tree Maker and then creating an address report that organizes them all.

This type of report can also be useful when creating mailing lists for family newsletters or making a list of relatives you want to send Christmas cards or wedding invitations to. You can include addresses, e-mail addresses, and even phone numbers.

Adding an Address for an Individual

Before you can generate an address report, you need to enter contact information for all the relevant individuals in your tree.

1. Go to the **Family** tab on the People workspace.

2. In the pedigree view or index click the name of the individual for whom you want to add an address.

3. Click the **Person** tab; then click the **Facts** button. The Individual and Shared Facts workspace opens.

4. Click the **Add Fact** (+) button in the toolbar. The Add Fact window opens.

5. Click "Address" in the **Facts** list and click **OK**.

Facts	Type		
Address	Individual		OK
Adoption	Individual		Cancel
Also Known As	Individual		
Ancestral File Number	Individual		Help
Annulment	Shared		
Arrival	Individual		New...
Baptism	Individual		
Baptism (LDS)	Individual		
Bar Mitzvah	Individual		
Bat Mitzvah	Individual		
Birth	Individual		
Blessing	Individual		
Burial	Individual		
Caste	Individual		
Cause of Death	Individual		
Census	Individual		
Christening	Individual		

6. In the individual's editing panel, enter the address in the **Place** field. If you want, you can repeat steps 4 through 6 and add the Phone Number and Email facts also.

Creating an Address Report

1. Open the **Custom Report** (located on the Publish workspace under Person Reports).

2. Click the **Reset** button in the reports toolbar to clear any previous report settings.

3. Click the **Items to include** button in the reports toolbar. The Items to Include window opens.

Now you'll add the Address fact to the report.

4. Click the blue (**+**) button. The Select Fact window opens.

5. Choose "Address" from the **Facts** list and click **OK**. You might want to repeat steps 4 and 5 to add the "Phone Number" and "Email" fact, also.

You'll now delete the other default facts that are included in the report.

6. In the **Included facts** list, highlight a fact, such as birth, and click the red (**X**) button.

Delete all the displayed facts except the contact information you want in the report.

7. Click **OK**.

Now you can choose who you want to include in the report. The quickest option is to simply include everyone in your tree by choosing "All individuals." However, you can refine the list if you want. In this example, I want to select all the descendants of my maternal grandparents.

8. In **Individuals to include**, click **Selected individuals**. The Filter Individuals window opens. No individuals should be included in the report at this point; if there are, click **Exclude All** to clear the report.

Filter Individuals				
Name:	◀ ▶			
Name	**Birth**		**Name**	**Birth**
(Hoyt), John Hait	24 Nov 1740	Include >		
(Shanklin), Permelia A.	Abt. 1814	Include All >>		
Adams, James		Ancestors >		
Bell, Abigail				
Bennington, Sarah	Abt. 1812	Descendants >		
Bobbitt, Alta M.	09 Feb 1892	Filter In... >		
Bobbitt, Arthur L.	24 Aug 1897			
Bobbitt, Bessie A.	14 Dec 1888			
Bobbitt, Charity M.	10 Mar 1883			
Bobbitt, Cornelia	Abt. 1856			
Bobbitt, Eugene A.	Jan 1877	< Exclude		
Bobbitt, Fern Edna	Apr 1909	<< Exclude All		
Bobbitt, Francis M.	Abt. 1869	< Filter Out...		
Bobbitt, Isham				
Bobbitt, James Clarence	28 Jul 1858			
Bobbitt, James Leslie	19 Sep 1884			
Bobbitt, Jessie	Abt. 1873			
Bobbitt, John W.	Jun 1832			

Individuals included in list: 271   Individuals included in filter: 0

OK   Cancel   Help

9. To choose a group of descendants, click an ancestor's name in the **Name** list (in this case, my grandmother).

10. Click **Descendants**. The list on the right side of the window now includes a list of that ancestor's descendants.

Now you can filter the list further to include only individuals for whom you've entered addresses.

11. Click **Filter Out**. The Filter Individuals by Criteria window opens.

12. Click **All facts**.

13. Choose "Address" and "Place" from the **Search where** drop-down list.

14. Choose "Is blank" from the next drop-down list.

Filter Individuals By Criteria	✕

○ Vital facts   ⊙ All facts   ○ Other

Search where: Value:

[Address ▾] [Is blank ▾] [   ]

[Place ▾]   ☐ Secondary facts   ⊙ Match all values   ○ Match any value

[OK] [Cancel] [Help]

15. Click **OK**. The Filter Individuals window now shows all the individuals for whom you have entered an address.

16. Click **OK**. The report opens.

Custom Report Preview

[🖑] [90% ▾] 🔍 🔍   ◀ ▶ ▶▌ [𝄖]

Address Report

Dehek, Steve J.
     Address: PO Box 173 Hyde Park, UT 84318-0173

Eddins, Faren Zane
     Address: 505 Indian Hills Dr. Moscow ID 83843-9355

Eddins, Lataun C.
     Address: 592 Crestview Ln Tetonia, ID 83452-5453

Eddins, Robert D.
     Address: 4223 E 540 N

Eddins, Roy
     Address: 40 S First E Bancroft, ID 83217-5149

Eddins, Val G.
     Address: 195 S First E Bancroft, ID 83217-5152

Mecham, Larry
     Address: 598 E 2300 N Monteview, ID 83435-5044

Mecham, Leroy S.
     Address: 1406 N 1200 E Shelley, ID 83274-5161

Mecham, Marci Loraine
     Address: PO Box 3584 Idaho Falls, ID 83403-3584

Mecham, Matthew Levi
     Address: 1450 E 1200 N Terreton, ID 83450-5100

Mecham, Melvin Leroy
     Address: 5312 Joe Ln Nampa, ID 83687-8780

Pedersen, Elray
     Address: 6250 Indian School Rd NE, Apt A204 Albuquerque, NM 87110-5377

Adoption

Traditionally, genealogy is used to track direct bloodlines. So how do adopted family members fit in? In most families, adopted children are as much a part of the family as any biological children and you'll want to include them in your family trees. If you do include adopted family members, make sure you clearly identify them as such. That way others who view your tree will have a clear picture of your family.

Adding an Adopted Individual to Your Tree

You have many options when adding an adopted individual to your tree. In this example, you'll learn how to enter two sets of parents for the individual—biological and legal.

1. Go to the **Family** tab on the People workspace.

2. In the pedigree view or family group view click the name of the adopted individual.

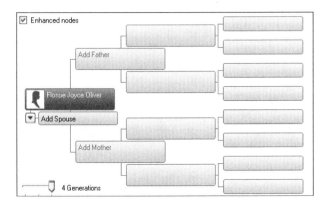

3. Click the **Add Father** and **Add Mother** buttons in the pedigree view and add the names of the individual's adopted parents.

4. Click the name of the adopted individual again.

5. Click the **Person** tab; then click the **Relationships** button.

6. Click the father or mother's name in the Relationships workspace.

7. In the editing panel, choose "Adopted" from the **Relationship** drop-down list. If both parents are the adoptive parents, complete steps 6 and 7 for each parent.

If you want to include information about the individual's biological parents, continue with these steps:

8. Without leaving the Relationships workspace, choose **Person>Add Person>Add Father**. The Add Father window opens.

9. Enter the biological father's name and click **OK**. The Relationships workspace opens.

10. In the editing panel, make sure "Natural" is displayed in the **Relationship** drop-down list.

11. In the mini pedigree tree above the workspace, click the **Add Spouse** button next to the father you just added. The Add Spouse window opens.

   Don't worry about this individual being labeled a "spouse." You'll define the parents' relationship in another step.

12. Enter the biological mother's name and click **OK**. The Relationships workspace opens.

13. In the editing panel, make sure "Natural" is displayed in the **Relationship** drop-down list.

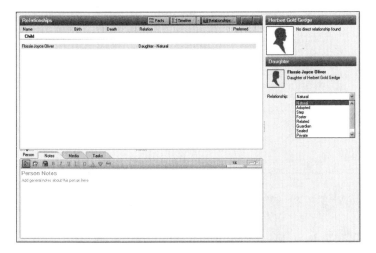

14. To change the default "Spouse" relationship for the parents, click the father's name in the Relationships workspace. In the editing panel, choose a relationship type, such as "Partner," from the **Relationship** drop-down list.

Now that you've entered both sets of parents for the adopted individual, you can choose the "preferred parents"—the parents you want displayed in charts, reports, and software views. Usually this would be the individual's direct ancestors; however, with adopted children you may choose to display their legal parents.

Choosing a Preferred Set of Parents

If you have entered two sets of parents for an adopted individual, you can choose which parents are the preferred parents, the parents who will be displayed in reports and charts.

1. Go to the **Family** tab on the **People** workspace.

2. In the pedigree view or index click the name of the adopted individual.

3. Click the **Person** tab; then click the **Relationships** button.

Under the "Fathers" and "Mothers" headings, you should see two sets of names, the natural and the adoptive parents.

4. Click the name of one of the parents you want to be displayed as the preferred parent; it doesn't matter whether you choose the father or the mother.

5. In the editing panel, click the **Preferred parent** checkbox. The Preferred Parents window opens.

Preferred Parents		✕
Preferred parents must be set as a pair.		
Select preferred parents for Flossie Joyce Oliver:		
Father	**Mother**	**P.**
Charles Harrison Oliver	Flossie Gold Gedge	P...
Herbert Gold Gedge	Sarah Hannah Gold	

☑ Update pedigree now   [OK] [Cancel] [Help]

6. Click a set of parents and click **OK**.

Entering Information About an Adoption

If you have adoption or court records pertaining to a family member's adoption, you'll want to enter these details into your tree.

1. Go to the **Family** tab on the People workspace.

2. In the pedigree view or index click the name of the individual you want to add information to.

3. Click the **Person** tab; then click the **Facts** button. The Individual and Shared Facts workspace opens.

4. Click the **Add Fact** (**+**) button in the toolbar. The Add Fact window opens.

5. Click "Adoption" in the **Facts** list and click **OK**.

6. In the individual's editing panel, enter any dates and places associated with the adoption in the necessary fields. Don't forget to add any sources you have.

Creating an Adoption Report

You can create a report of all the individuals in your tree whom you have identified as adopted.

1. Open the **Custom Report** (located on the Publish workspace under Person Reports).

2. Click the **Reset** button in the reports toolbar to clear any previous report settings.

3. In **Individuals to include**, click **Selected individuals**. The Filter Individuals window opens. No individuals should be included in the report at this point; if there are, click **Exclude All** to clear the report.

4. Click **Filter In**. The Filter Individuals by Criteria window opens.

5. Click **Other**.

6. Choose "Child Relationship Types" from the **Search where** drop-down list.

7. Choose "Equals" from the next drop-down list.

8. Choose "Adopted" from the **Value** drop-down list.

9. Click **OK**. The Filter Individuals window now shows all the individuals whom you have identified as adopted. You can further filter the list if necessary.

10. Click **OK**.

Now the report shows the individuals who have been designated as adopted. If you also want to include adoption facts in the report, follow these steps:

11. Click the **Items to include** button in the reports toolbar. The Items to Include window opens.

12. Click the blue (+) button. The Select Fact window opens.

13. Choose "Adoption" from the **Facts** list.

You can delete the other facts included in the report, if necessary.

14. In the **Included facts** list, highlight a fact, such as birth, and click the red (**X**) button.

Delete all the displayed facts that you don't want except the Adoption fact.

15. Click **OK**. The report opens.

All-in-One Report

The all-in-one report is an alphabetical list of every family member you have entered in a tree—even if the only information you've entered is a name. The report can be quite long, especially if you have a large number of people in your tree. In this example, only names and birth, marriage, and death dates are included; however, you can choose any facts you'd like.

1. Open the **Custom Report** (located on the Publish workspace under Person Reports).

2. Click the **Reset** button in the reports toolbar to clear any previous report settings.

3. In **Individuals to include,** click **All individuals**. The report opens.

Custom Report Preview

81%

All-in-One Report

(Hoyt), John Hait
Birth: 24 Nov 1740
Marriage: 31 Dec 1761
Death: 01 Mar 1825
Bell, Abigail
Marriage: Bet. 08 Mar 1738–1739
Bell, Permelia A.
Birth: Abt. 1814 in Kentucky
Marriage: Bet. 1861–1870
Bennington, Constance
Birth: 1806 in Boone County, Kentucky, USA
Death: Apr 1842
Bennington, Mary Elizabeth
Bennington, Sarah
Birth: Abt. 1812 in Kentucky
Marriage: 21 Mar 1837 in Fulton, Illinois
Death: 13 Aug 1863 in Marshall County, Illinois
Bennington, William Jr.
Marriage: 16 Apr 1793 in Bourbon County, Kentucky, USA
Bobbitt, Alta M.
Birth: 09 Feb 1892 in Kansas
Death: 04 Nov 1987
Bobbitt, Arthur L.
Birth: 24 Aug 1897 in Oklahoma
Death: May 1982
Bobbitt, Cornelia

Page 1 of 14   Zoom Factor: 81%

Ancestry.com Family Trees

If you're like me, you have kept your family trees in various locations over the years—my first experimental tree on WorldConnect at RootsWeb, a tree for sharing on Ancestry.com, and my main "working" Family Tree Maker database, which resides on my laptop. And I'll admit that I haven't been diligent about updating my various trees and making sure they all contain the same information. At this point I have facts and sources in my Ancestry tree that aren't included in my main Family Tree Maker database. Ancestry.com doesn't have the functionality to let me sync my two trees together, but I can quickly download my Ancestry tree in Family Tree Maker and either keep it as a separate tree or merge it with one of my existing files.

When you download your Ancestry tree, it will include all the facts, sources, and images you have manually attached to individuals. If you have linked Ancestry.com records to your tree, the downloaded tree will include only the information and sources associated with the records, not the actual record images.

> You do not need a subscription to Ancestry.com to create a family tree, but you do have to be a registered member.

1. Go to the **New Tree** tab on the Plan workspace.

2. Make sure you are logged in to your Ancestry.com account. If you aren't, you can log in by clicking the **Login** link on the Web Dashboard.

In order to download an Ancestry tree, you must be the tree's owner; even if you have been invited to view or share a tree, you will not be able to download the file. If you do find a tree you want to download but don't have rights to it, consider using the Ancestry Connection service to politely request that the owner download a GEDCOM of it for you.

3. Click **Download a tree from Ancestry**. A list of your trees appears.

Trees	Date Modified	Download
Ancestry Press	3/10/2008	Download
Descendants of Maurine Bobbitt	7/30/2007	Download
Lord Family Tree	3/10/2008	Download
Pedersen Family	6/19/2009	Download
Pedersen-Reed	6/13/2009	Download
Shepard Family Tree	4/1/2009	Download

4. Click the **Download** button next to the tree you want to download. A message asks you whether you want to merge the Ancestry tree with an existing tree or create a new one.

5. Click **Import** to save the file as a new tree; click **Merge** to merge the file with an existing tree.

If you choose to import the tree, you will be prompted to enter a name for the tree and save it; if you choose to merge the file with an existing tree, the Merge Wizard will open and guide you through merging the trees. A message tells you when the process is complete.

Cemetery Report

For an upcoming Memorial Day celebration, I plan on visiting a nearby cemetery where at least fifteen family members are buried. I want to take a photo of each tombstone to include in my tree and also compare dates with the information I already have. In anticipation of the event, I have created a custom cemetery report that shows the names (and dates) of every family member buried in that cemetery. I'll take the report with me so I won't have to rely on my own memory and perhaps miss someone.

Entering Burial Information for an Individual

Before you can generate a cemetery report, you need to enter burial information for all the relevant individuals in your tree.

1. Go to the **Family** tab on the People workspace.

2. In the pedigree view or index click the name of the individual for whom you want to add a burial fact.

3. Click the **Person** tab; then click the **Facts** button. The Individual and Shared Facts workspace opens.

4. Click the **Add Fact** (+) button in the toolbar. The Add Fact window opens.

5. Click "Burial" in the **Facts** list and click **OK**.

Facts	Type
Address	Individual
Adoption	Individual
Also Known As	Individual
Ancestral File Number	Individual
Annulment	Shared
Arrival	Individual
Baptism	Individual
Baptism (LDS)	Individual
Bar Mitzvah	Individual
Bat Mitzvah	Individual
Birth	Individual
Blessing	Individual
Burial	Individual
Caste	Individual
Cause of Death	Individual
Census	Individual
Christening	Individual

OK | Cancel | Help | New...

6. In the individual's editing panel, enter the name of the cemetery in the **Place** or **Description** field. Don't forget to add any sources you have.

Creating a Cemetery Report

You can create a report of all the individuals in your tree who were buried in the same cemetery.

1. Open the **Custom Report** (located on the Publish workspace under Person Reports).

2. Click the **Reset** button in the reports toolbar to clear any previous report settings.

3. In **Individuals to include**, click **Selected individuals**. The Filter Individuals window opens. No individuals should be included in the report at this point; if there are, click **Exclude All** to clear the report.

4. Click **Filter In**. The Filter Individuals by Criteria window opens.

5. Click **All facts**.

6. Choose "Burial" from the **Search where** drop-down list; then choose "Place" or "Description." The field you choose depends on where you've entered the cemetery name.

7. Choose "Contains" from the next drop-down list.

8. In the **Value** field, enter the name of the cemetery. Make sure you enter the cemetery name exactly as you've entered it in the Burial fact.

9. Click **OK**. The Filter Individuals window now shows all the individuals who are buried in a particular cemetery.

10. Click **OK**.

Now the report shows the individuals who have been buried in the designated cemetery. If you want to include the Burial fact in the report, follow these steps:

11. Click the **Items to include** button in the reports toolbar. The Items to Include window opens.

12. Click the blue (+) button. The Select Fact window opens.

13. Choose "Burial" from the **Facts** list.

You can delete the other facts included in the report (for example, you may not need to include the Marriage fact).

14. To delete a fact from the report, highlight a fact, such as marriage, in the **Included facts** list, and click the red (**X**) button.

15. Click **OK**. The report opens.

Childless Individuals

If you determine that an individual or couple in your family tree never had children you might want to record this fact somewhere in your tree. This helpful tidbit can save other family researchers from spending time on fruitless searches for nonexistent children and records.

I have two maiden aunts who lived together their entire lives, never marrying or having children. One option was to record this information by simply entering it in a person note for each aunt. Although this would have been an adequate solution, I decided to create a custom "No descendants" fact. Facts give you an advantage because they allow you to include source information and you don't have to worry that the information will get lost at the bottom of a note. In addition, you can include facts on any reports or charts you create.

Once you have created a fact, you can use it for anyone in your family tree if you discover he or she has no offspring. To learn how to create a custom "No descendants" fact, see "Custom Facts."

Colorful Charts

What family historian doesn't want to brag a little about their latest find or display their hard work for all to see? And one of the easiest ways to showcase your family is with charts. Family Tree Maker lets you easily create a variety of standard ancestor and descendant charts, but with a little effort (and practice) you can make charts that add some color and personality to your history. You can change colors and box styles by gender, generations, ancestral lines, and more.

Because each Family Tree Maker chart is a little different and you can use a wide variety of formatting options, I recommend spending some time playing around with the software using the basic guidelines explained here. It may take a little practice before you get the results you want.

Selecting People in a Chart

Before you change the chart's formatting, you'll want to learn how to select groups of individuals to work with.

1. Access the chart you want to work with (on the Detail tab of the Publish workspace). In this example I'll be working with the 180 Fan Chart.

2. Right-click an individual's name in the chart. A drop-down list lets you choose whom to include in your group (e.g., ancestors, descendants, individuals of the same generation).

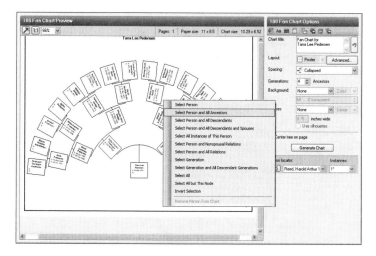

Because I want each of the four branches of my tree to be a different color, I'll start with my maternal grandfather and click his name in the chart and choose "Select Person and All Ancestors." The individuals who are selected currently are highlighted in blue.

You can also select individuals by pressing the CTRL key and clicking on each person you want to include in the group. For me, this is an efficient way to create a group, and I always know exactly who is being excluded and included.

3. After you've selected the individuals you want for a group, right-click the chart again and choose **Mark Selected>Marking 1**. This indicates to Family Tree Maker that you want to change the selected individuals as a group.

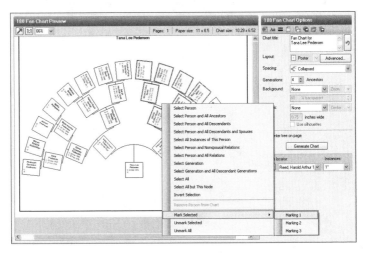

4. Using steps 2 and 3, you can create multiple groups. As you create additional groups, make sure you designate the second group as "Marking 2" and the third group as "Marking 3." If you choose "Marking 1" for each group, every group will have the same formatting.

> If you accidentally select an individual you don't want to include in a group, you can right-click the individual's box on the chart and choose **Unmark Selected** from the drop-down list.

After you've marked your groups, you're ready to choose their formatting.

Changing Chart Formatting for a Group

You can change the box borders, colors, lines, and fonts for each group you've created.

1. In the Chart Options editing toolbar, click the **Box and line styles** button. The Box, Border, and Line Options window opens.

2. In Boxes, choose "Marked Boxes 1" from the drop-down list (this is first group of individuals you selected).

3. Make any formatting changes you'd like for the group. In my chart I'll change the fill color for each branch of my tree.

4. In Boxes, choose "Marked Boxes 2" from the drop-down list and make any necessary formatting changes for the group. Then do the same for the "Marked Boxes 3" group.

5. Click **OK**.

6. If you want to you can choose which facts are included in the report by clicking the **Items to include** button in the chart editing toolbar. In my example only names are included.

Here's an example of my 180 Fan chart, which uses a different color for each family line.

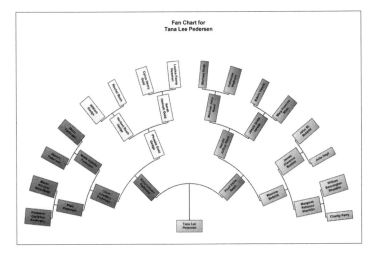

Custom Facts

Family Tree Maker has a variety of default facts you use when entering information about your family. However, some of the details you gather don't always fit into these defined categories. You could enter this information into a personal note for the individual. But before you do, consider making a custom fact. When you add information to an individual as a fact rather than a note, you can assign dates and places and attach sources, and you can include the fact in reports and charts.

I have created several custom facts, such as "Died as an Infant," that I use quite a bit. Here are a few suggestions for some custom facts you might want to add to your trees:

- Cemetery Record
- Civil Union
- Died as Infant
- Godparent
- Hobbies
- No Descendants or Never Had Children
- Number of Children
- Obituary
- Migration
- Moved
- Notes
- Tombstones
- Unmarried
- Witness
- Wars

You might also want to create a fact for each specific census year or for specific wars (such as the Civil War, American Revolution, or Korean War).

Adding a Custom Fact to a Tree

1. Click **Edit>Manage Facts**. The Manage Facts window opens.

2. Click **New**. The Add Custom Fact window opens.

Add Custom Fact

Fact label:

Short label:

Abbreviation:

Fact type
- ⊙ Individual fact
- ○ Shared fact

Fact elements
- ⊙ Date / Place
- ○ Date / Place / Description
- ○ Description only

OK   Cancel   Help

3. In the **Fact label** field, enter the name of the fact as it will appear on the Person tab and on charts and reports.

4. In the **Short label** field, enter a short label for the fact that will appear on the Family tab editing panel; you can enter up to six characters.

5. In the **Abbreviation** field, enter an abbreviation for the fact; you can enter up to three characters.

6. In **Fact type**, choose whether this fact will be used for individual events or shared events. Individual facts apply to only one person, such as the "Unmarried" fact; shared facts are typically events like marriage or divorce that occur between two people, usually spouses. In my list of custom facts, "Civil Union" would be a shared fact.

7. In **Fact elements**, choose the fields that you want to appear for the fact: Date and Place; Date, Place, and Description; or Description only. For example, for a custom Notes fact, you'd probably choose to have only a description, but for a Civil War fact, you'd want to include a date, place, and description.

8. Click **OK**.

Adding a Custom Fact to an Individual

Now that you've added a custom fact to your tree, you can add it to a specific person.

1. Go to the **Family** tab on the **People** workspace.

2. In the pedigree view or index click the name of the individual for whom you want to add the fact.

3. Click the **Person** tab; then click the **Facts** button. The Individual and Shared Facts workspace opens.

4. Click the **Add Fact** (**+**) button in the toolbar. The Add Fact window opens.

Add Fact		
Facts	**Type**	OK
Confirmation	Individual	Cancel
Confirmation (LDS)	Individual	Help
Cremation	Individual	
Death	Individual	New...
Degree	Individual	
Departure	Individual	
Died as Infant	Individual	
Divorce	Shared	
Divorce Filed	Shared	
DNA Markers	Individual	
Education	Individual	
Elected	Individual	
Email	Individual	
Emigration	Individual	
Employment	Individual	
Endowment (LDS)	Individual	
Engagement	Shared	

5. Click the custom fact in the **Facts** list and click **OK**.

6. In the individual's editing panel, complete the date, place, or description for the fact.

Customizing the Index Panel

It's easy to get in the habit of opening Family Tree Maker, entering data, and closing the program without really thinking. But if you take a few minutes to change your preferences or tweak settings that are compatible with how *you* work, you might be surprised at how much more efficiently your data entry goes.

The People workspace is the place where you will spend most of your time in Family Tree Maker. And the Index panel on the Family tab is your key to displaying the individuals and family lines you want to focus on. You can determine how names are displayed, add dates, and sort by a variety of options.

Changing Name Displays in the Index

You can change your name preferences for the Index panel. You can include titles, alternate names, and married names for females.

1. Click **Tools**>**Options**. The Options window opens.

2. Click the **Dates/Names** tab.

3. If you have entered names for individuals in the Also Known As fact, click the **Use AKA if available after middle name** checkbox to have these alternate names included with the preferred name (for example, Bobbitt, Mary Eliza "Mollie").

4. If you have entered names for individuals in the Also Known As fact, click the **Use AKA if available as an additional entry** checkbox to have these alternate names appear as their own entries in the Index panel (for example, Hannah "Anna" Willis and Anna Willis).

5. If you have entered titles for individuals in the Title fact, click the **Use titles if available** checkbox to have the titles included with the preferred name (for example, Hait, Captain Samuel).

6. If you want a woman's married name included—in addition to her maiden name—click the **Use married names for females** checkbox (for example, Hoyt, Maria Hitchcock).

7. Click **OK**.

Displaying Dates in the Index

If—like me—you have a tree full of Sams, Elizabeths, and Marys (all with the same surname, of course) you might want to add birth, death, or marriage dates to the Index panel display so that it's easier to distinguish between them.

1. Go to the **Family** tab on the **People** workspace.

2. Click the **Show additional data** button in the upper-right corner of the panel.

3. From the drop-down list, choose to add birth, marriage, or death dates to the Index.

Changing the Sort Order in the Index

Names in the Index can be sorted alphabetically by name (given or surname) and by date (birth, marriage, and death).

1. Go to the **Family** tab on the **People** workspace.

2. From the **Sort** drop-down list, choose how you want to sort the names. If you choose to sort by date, you will see sub-headings grouping the names together.

Divorce

Even today, divorce can strain family relationships and bonds. You may be reluctant to include information about these marriages, especially if the union didn't produce any children. However, each detail you learn about a person can lead you to new records and new information. Also, these events complete the picture of what your ancestor's life was really like. If you are concerned about this information appearing in reports and charts, remember that you can choose to include or exclude people and facts in most of these. Also, when you export your files, you can choose to exclude facts you've marked as private.

Changing a Marital Status to Divorced

If a marriage ends in divorce, you'll want to record this change in your tree.

> This task shows you how to change the status of a marriage that has already been entered in your tree. If you haven't already, you'll need to add the couple to your tree and record their marriage information.

1. Go to the **Family** tab on the **People** workspace.

2. Click the name of the individual whose marital status you want to change.

3. Click the **Person** tab; then click the **Relationships** button.

4. Click the spouse's name in the Relationships workspace.

5. In the editing panel, choose "Divorced" from the **Status** drop-down list.

Entering Information About a Divorce

If you have court records, divorce decrees, or other records pertaining to an individual's divorce, you'll want to enter these details into your tree.

1. Go to the People workspace and click the **Person** tab for the individual you want to add information for.

2. Click the **Facts** button. The Individual and Shared Facts workspace opens.

3. Click the **Add Fact** (+) button in the toolbar. The Add Fact window opens.

Add Fact

Facts	Type
Death	Individual
Degree	Individual
Departure	Individual
Divorce	Shared
Divorce Filed	Shared
DNA Markers	Individual
Education	Individual
Elected	Individual
Email	Individual
Emigration	Individual
Employment	Individual
Endowment (LDS)	Individual
Engagement	Shared
Excommunication	Individual
First Communion	Individual
Funeral	Individual
Graduation	Individual

OK
Cancel
Help

New...

4. Click "Divorce" in the **Facts** list and click **OK**.

5. In the individual's editing panel, choose the divorced spouse's name and enter any dates and places associated with the divorce in the necessary fields. Don't forget to add any sources you have.

Creating a Divorce Report

You can create a report of all the individuals in your tree who have been divorced.

1. Open the **Custom Report** (located on the Publish workspace under Person Reports).

2. Click the **Reset** button in the reports toolbar to clear any previous report settings.

3. In **Individuals to include**, click **Selected individuals**. The Filter Individuals window opens. No individuals should be included in the report at this point; if there are, click **Exclude All** to clear the report.

4. Click **Filter In**. The Filter Individuals by Criteria window opens.

5. Click **Other**.

6. Choose "Relationship Status" from the **Search where** drop-down list.

7. Choose "Equals" from the next drop-down list.

8. Choose "Divorced" from the **Value** drop-down list.

9. Click **OK**. The Filter Individuals window now shows all the individuals you have identified as divorced. You can filter the list further if necessary.

10. Click **OK**.

Now the report shows the individuals who have been designated as divorced. If you also want to include divorce details in the report, follow these steps:

11. Click the **Items to include** button in the reports toolbar. The Items to Include window opens.

12. Click the blue (+) button. The Select Fact window opens.

13. Choose "Divorce" from the **Facts** list.

You can delete the other facts included in the report, if necessary.

14. In the **Included facts** list, highlight a fact, such as birth, and click the red (**X**) button.

Delete the other displayed facts except the Divorce fact.

15. Click **OK**. The report opens.

Editing an Individual

Maybe this has happened to you: you're looking at a pedigree chart and realize that you've reversed your grandfather's birth date and month, or perhaps while you're viewing the migration path for an uncle you notice that a location is missing. Instead of leaving the area where you're working to edit the individual, you now have the flexibility to edit facts, write notes, and add media items from every workspace.

Editing in the Places Workspace

1. While in the Places workspace, choose "Person" from the **List by** drop-down list.

2. Right-click a name and choose **Edit Person**.

In the Places workspace, you can also right-click on the individual's name in the right panel to open the Edit Person window.

Editing in the Media Workspace

1. While in the Media workspace, choose "Person" from the **List by** drop-down list.

2. Right-click a name and choose **Edit Person**.

Editing in the Sources Workspace

1. While in the Sources workspace, choose "Person" from the **List by** drop-down list.

2. Right-click a name and choose **Edit Person**.

In the Sources workspace, you can also right-click the individual's name on the Links tab at the bottom of the window to open the Edit Person window.

Editing in the Publish Workspace

1. While in a chart or report on the Publish workspace, right-click the individual's name in the mini pedigree tree below the main toolbar and choose **Edit Person**.

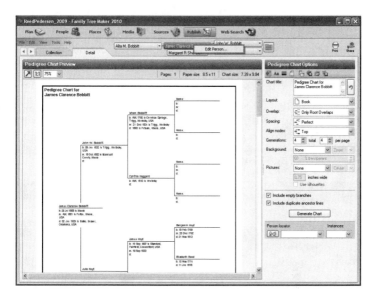

You can also double-click an individual's name in a chart to open the Edit Person window.

Exporting Files

When sharing Family Tree Maker trees with family members, you may want to create a file that includes only certain individuals. I am creating a website about my mother's ancestry that I want to upload a GEDCOM to. Because my current Family Tree Maker tree contains both sides of my family, I'm going to create a new GEDCOM by exporting only my maternal ancestors. That way family members accessing the website will see a family tree that includes only people they are directly related to.

Exporting a Maternal Ancestors File

1.   Choose **File>Export**. The Export window opens.

2.   Click **Selected individuals**. The Filter Individuals window opens. No individuals should be included in the export at this point; if there are, click **Exclude All** to clear the export.

3. Click your mother's name in the **Name** list.

4. Click **Ancestors**. The list on the right side of the window now includes all your maternal ancestors. Keep in mind that these are your direct ancestors. If you want to include your ancestors' siblings, you'll need to manually add them. One easy way to do this is by surname.

5. Click **Filter In**. The Filter Individuals by Criteria window opens.

6. Click **Vital facts**.

7. Choose "Name" from the **Search where** drop-down list.

8. Choose "Contains" from the next drop-down list.

9. In the **Value** field, enter a surname.

10. Click **OK**. The list now contains your direct maternal ancestors and individuals with a specific surname. Repeat steps 5 through 10 until all the individuals you want included are in the list.

11. Click **OK** on the Filter Individuals window. The Export window reopens.

12. In **Output format,** choose whether you are creating a GED-COM or a Family Tree Maker file and choose any other options as necessary.

13. Click **OK**. The Export To window opens.

14. In the **Save in** field, choose the location where the exported file will be saved.

15. Click **Save**. A message tells you when your file has been exported successfully.

Family Tree Maker automatically names the exported file with the same name as the current tree. If you want to use a different name, you can change it in the File name field.

Exporting a Paternal Ancestors File

1. Choose **File>Export**. The Export window opens.

2. Click **Selected individuals**. The Filter Individuals window opens. No individuals should be included in the export at this point; if there are, click **Exclude All** to clear the export.

3. Click your father's name in the **Name** list.

4. Click **Ancestors**. The list on the right side of the window now includes all your paternal ancestors. Keep in mind that these are your direct ancestors. If you want to include your ancestors' siblings, you'll need to manually add them. One easy way to do this is by surname.

5. Click **Filter In**. The Filter Individuals by Criteria window opens.

6. Click **Vital facts**.

7. Choose "Name" from the **Search where** drop-down list.

8. Choose "Contains" from the next drop-down list.

9. In the **Value** field, enter a surname.

10. Click **OK**. The list now contains your direct paternal ancestors and individuals with a specific surname. Repeat steps 5 through 10 until all the individuals you want included are in the list.

11. Click **OK**. The Export window reopens.

12. In **Output format,** choose whether you are creating a GEDCOM or a Family Tree Maker file and choose any other options as necessary.

13. Click **OK**. The Export To window opens.

14. In the **Save in** field, choose the location where the exported file will be saved.

Family Tree Maker automatically names the exported file with the same name as the current tree. If you want to use a different name, you can change it in the File name field.

15. Click **Save**. A message tells you when your file has been exported successfully.

Family Health Histories

In 2004, the Surgeon General's office launched the Family Health Initiative and encouraged everyone to create a family health history. Knowing this type of information can help you know what diseases you are at risk for and perhaps help you prevent illnesses that run in family lines. According to the Surgeon General, the six most useful hereditary diseases to track are (1) heart disease, (2) stroke, (3) diabetes, (4) colon cancer, (5) breast cancer, and (6) ovarian cancer.

One great resource for medical information is death certificates. Recently I obtained sixteen death certificates for one branch of my family. Each one listed a cause of death and many included contributing factors. Family Tree Maker made it easy for me to record all this information and run a quick report. If you have gathered health information about your family members you might want to give a family health history a try.

Adding Medical Information for an Individual

Before you can generate a family health history, you need to enter causes of death and medical conditions for all the relevant individuals in your tree.

1. Go to the **Family** tab on the **People** workspace.

2. In the pedigree view or index click the name of the individual for whom you want to add medical information.

3. Click the **Person** tab; then click the **Facts** button. The Individual and Shared Facts workspace opens.

4. Click the **Add Fact** (+) button in the toolbar. The Add Fact window opens.

5. Click "Cause of Death" in the **Facts** list and click **OK**.

Facts	Type		
Blessing	Individual		OK
Burial	Individual		
Caste	Individual		Cancel
Cause of Death	Individual		
Census	Individual		Help
Christening	Individual		
Christening (adult)	Individual		New...
Circumcision	Individual		
Civil	Individual		
Confirmation	Individual		
Confirmation (LDS)	Individual		
Cremation	Individual		
Death	Individual		
Degree	Individual		
Departure	Individual		
Died as Infant	Individual		
Divorce	Shared		

6. In the individual's editing panel, enter the cause of death in the **Description** field. If you want, you can repeat steps 4 through 6 and add the Medical Condition fact.

Creating a Family Health History Report

1. Open the **Custom Report** (located on the Publish workspace under Person Reports).

2. Click the **Reset** button in the reports toolbar to clear any previous report settings.

3. Click the **Items to include** button in the reports toolbar. The Items to Include window opens.

Now you'll add the medical facts to the report.

4. Click the blue (+) button. The Select Fact window opens.

5. Choose "Cause of Death" from the **Facts** list.

6. Click **OK**. You might want to repeat steps 4 through 6 to add the Medical Condition fact too.

You can now delete any facts you don't want to include in the report.

7. In the **Included facts** list, highlight a fact, such as birth, and click the red button.

8. Click **OK**. The report is displayed. If you want the report to display only individuals in your tree who have medical conditions and causes of death recorded, continue with the following steps:

9. In **Individuals to include**, click **Selected individuals**. The Filter Individuals window opens. No individuals should be included in the report at this point; if there are, click **Exclude All** to clear the report.

10. Click **Filter In**. The Filter Individuals by Criteria window opens.

11. Click **All facts**.

12. Choose "Cause of Death" from the **Search where** drop-down list; then choose "Description."

13. Choose "Is not blank" from the next drop-down list.

14. Click **OK**. The Filter Individuals window now shows all the individuals who have recorded causes of death. We'll now add those who have recorded medical conditions.

15. Click **Filter In**. The Filter Individuals by Criteria window opens.

16. Click **All facts**.

17. Choose "Medical Condition" from the **Search where** drop-down list; then choose "Description."

Filter Individuals By Criteria

○ Vital facts ● All facts ○ Other

Search where:

| Medical Condition ▾ | Is not blank ▾ | Value: |

| Description ▾ | ☐ Secondary facts | ● Match all values | ○ Match any value |

[OK] [Cancel] [Help]

18. Choose "Is not blank" from the next drop-down list.

19. Click **OK** on the Filter Individuals by Criteria window.

20. Click **OK** again. The report opens.

Custom Report Preview

81% ▾ ⊝ ⊕ | ◄ ◄ ► ►| | ▣

Family Health History

Abraham John Gold
Cause of Death: Smallpox
Anna Gedge
Cause of Death: Coronary ???
Cyrus Henry Gold
Cause of Death: Chronic myocarditis; chonric nephritis
Cyrus William Gold
Cause of Death: Cerebral hemorrhage
Flossie Gold Gedge
Cause of Death: Post partum hemorrhage; cerebral embolism
Herbert Gedge
Cause of Death: Cerebral hemorrhage
Herbert Gold Gedge
Cause of Death: Diptheria
Lorilla Gedge
Cause of Death: Mitral stenosis
Mary Willis
Cause of Death: Chronic rheumatoid arthritis
Phoebe Gold Gedge
Cause of Death: Cerebral hemorrhage
Rachel Bush
Cause of Death: Chronic valvular heart disease
Sarah Anna Gedge
Cause of Death: Septicemia; acute endocarditis
Sarah Thompson

Finding a Tree File

I often—probably too often—find myself rearranging my computer files: creating new folders, regrouping documents by subject, and moving items from desktop to folders. One problem though, sometimes my reorganization causes me to "lose" files. If you can't find your Family Tree Maker file, don't despair; you can use the Windows searching tool to quickly locate it, or any FTM backups you've created.

1. Click the **Start** button on the Windows taskbar; then select **Search**. The Search Results window opens.

2. In the search options panel, click the "Documents" link.

What do you want to search for?

→ Pictures, music, or video

→ Documents (word processing, spreadsheet, etc.)

→ All files and folders

→ Printers, computers, or people

② Information in Help and Support Center

You may also want to...

🔍 Search the Internet

☑ Change preferences

3. In the **All or part of the document name** field, enter ".ftm". Make sure you include the period before "ftm". That way your results will include files with the .ftm extension—not every file that has the letters FTM in it. If you want to search for your backup Family Tree Maker files, enter ".ftmb".

The Search Results window shows all the files that match your entry.

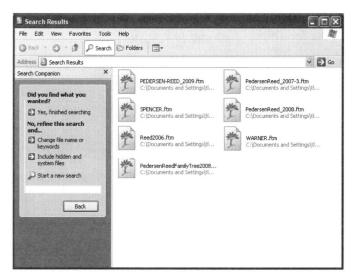

You can double-click the icon to open the file, or you can hover your mouse over the file name to see the file's location, size, and the date it was modified last. Make sure to take note of the file's location so you can find it in the future.

Foreign Language Characters

Many of us have ancestors from foreign countries, and in our research we come across names and places that use special characters (such as ø, ú, ö, and ñ). Family Tree Maker has a tool to help you enter the most common characters. You can also use the Character Map utility that comes with your Windows system to choose from hundreds of characters and symbols.

Entering a Character Using Family Tree Maker

1. On the People workspace, place your cursor in the field where you want to insert the character.

2. Click **Edit>Insert Symbol**. The Symbol window opens.

Symbol											☒
À	Á	Â	Ã	Ä	Å	Æ	ß	Ç			¿
È	É	Ê	Ë	Ì	Í	Î	Ī	Ñ			
Ò	Ó	Ô	Õ	Ö	Ø	Ù	Ú	Û	Ü	Ý	Ÿ
à	á	â	ā	ä	å	æ		ç			
è	é	ê	ë	ì	í	î	ī	ñ			
ò	ó	ô	õ	ö	ø	ù	ú	û	ü	ý	ÿ

Shortcut key: Alt+0192   [Insert]   [Close]   [Help]

3. Click the character you want to use; then click **Insert**.

Entering a Character Using the Character Map

Before you begin, make sure Family Tree Maker is open and you have your tree open to where you want to use the special character.

1. Click the **Start** button on the Windows taskbar; then select **All Programs**>**Accessories**>**System Tools**>**Character Map**. The Character Map opens.

If you do not find the Character Map under "All Programs," you can use the Windows Search tool to find it.

2. Use the scrollbar to find the character you want.

3. Click the character; then click **Select**. The character will appear in the Characters to copy field.

4. Click **Copy**.

5. Access your Family Tree Maker tree.

6. Place your cursor in the field where you want to insert the character.

7. Click **Edit**>**Paste**. The character is entered.

Global Searching

Have you ever entered important information in a note, but you can't remember whose it was? Or have you accidentally spelled an ancestor's name incorrectly throughout your tree? I make these types of mistakes on a regular basis. Luckily Family Tree Maker has a Find and Replace tool that lets you search for specific terms and names in facts, individual notes, media captions and descriptions, to-do tasks, and sources. In addition to searching, the tool also lets you replace any incorrect terms.

In my tree, I have a tendency to transpose the I and E in my great-grandfather's name, making him Neils instead of Niels. Instead of sifting through every fact, source, and media item for the incorrect spelling, I can use the tool to find the mistakes and correct them.

1. Choose **Edit>Find and Replace**. The Find and Replace window opens.

2. In the **Find** field, enter the term(s) you want to search for and click the **Find** button.

3. Change the search options, as necessary. You can choose how exact you want the search to be and which software elements to search. In this situation I want to search all elements because I am looking for a misspelled name. If you know the term you're looking for is in a source or a note, you can select only that option.

The window expands and shows the first item that matches your search.

Find And Replace

Find: neils

Replace with:

Options
- [ ] Match case
- [✓] Find whole words only
- [ ] Use wildcards (*?)

Search in
- [✓] Facts
- [✓] Notes
- [✓] Sources
- [✓] Media
- [✓] Tasks
- [✓] Places

Find Next

Replace All

Found in the person note(s) for Mette Katrina PEDERSEN (1860 - 1948)

Go To

Person note:
Mette came from Denmark with the children. Neils came to America approximately six months earlier.

Replace

Close

Help

4. If you want to open the record or workspace where the search term is used, click the **Go To** button.

5. If you want to replace the term, enter a new term in the **Replace with** field and click the **Replace** button.

6. To find the next matching term, click **Find Next**.

7. Continue searching and replacing terms, as necessary.

Although you can replace all matching search results by clicking the Replace All button, I recommend taking the time to view each specific search result and replace its content individually. For example, if I had chosen "Replace All" when searching for my great-grandfather's name, the tool would have changed his name in a source citation which I had transcribed directly from a record. In this instance, I want to keep the name as I found it.

If you do choose to use the Replace All functionality, you should back up your file first because you cannot undo these changes.

Group Deletion

In general, most people don't have a reason to delete a group of people from their tree. However, you might receive a file that contains a family you aren't related to or that you don't want to keep in your tree. You can use a couple techniques to delete them all at once. One option is to select a group to delete using a family tree chart. A second option is to export your tree and exclude the individuals you don't want in your file. You'll have a brand new Family Tree Maker 2010 file that includes all your media items, sources, and people—except those you've chosen to delete.

Instead of deleting a group of individuals, you might want to leave them in your tree and detach them from the people they're linked too. That way if you ever find a connection, you can simply reattach this branch to the appropriate member of your family, and you won't have to re-enter any information.

This section explains how to delete individuals from your tree and how to detach a group of individuals from your tree.

Warning: Deleting individuals from a tree is permanent. You should create a backup of your tree before deleting anyone.

Deleting a Group of People Using a Chart

Because Family Tree Maker contains a variety of charts and there are multiple ways to select individuals within these charts, this task includes only basic instructions. I recommend experimenting with the available chart selection tools and using them to delete individuals from your file.

1. Go to the **Collection** tab on the Publish workspace.

2. Click the name of the individual whom you want to be the focus of the chart in the mini-navigation pedigree tree or click the **Index of Individuals** button and choose a person.

3. Double-click the chart that will best display the group of people you want to delete. (The Extended Family Chart can be useful because it can display specific individuals or every individual in your tree.) Don't worry if individuals you don't want to delete appear in the chart; you can use the selection tools to further refine your choices.

4. To select specific individuals or groups to delete, right-click an individual's name in the chart. A drop-down list lets you choose specific groups to include (e.g., ancestors, descendants, individuals of the same generation). For more information on selecting groups of individuals, select **Help>Help for Family Tree Maker**.

You can also delete every person displayed in the chart by right-clicking the chart and selecting **Delete from File>All Persons in Chart** from the drop-down list.

5. After you have selected the group of individuals you want to delete, right-click one of the highlighted boxes and select **Delete from File>Selected Persons** from the drop-down list.

> You can also select specific individuals by pressing the CTRL key and clicking on each person you want to highlight in the group. For me, this is an efficient way to create a group, and I always know exactly who is being excluded and included.

Excluding Individuals from an Exported Tree

1. Choose **File>Export**. The Export window opens.

2. Click **Selected individuals**. The Filter Individuals window opens. No individuals should be included in the export at this point; if there are, click **Exclude All** to clear the export.

3. Click **Include All** to include every person in your tree in the exported file. The list on the right side of the window shows everyone in your tree. You can now "delete" individuals from the tree by excluding specific individuals or groups.

4. To remove a specific individual from your file, click the individual's name in the list on the right side of the window and click **Exclude**.

5. To exclude a group of people, click **Filter Out**. The Filter Individuals by Criteria window opens.

You can filter out individuals using several types of facts. In this example, we'll filter using a surname.

6. Click **Vital facts**.

7. Choose "Name" from the **Search where** drop-down list.

8. Choose "Contains" from the next drop-down list.

9. In the **Value** field, enter a surname.

10. Click **OK**. The list now contains everyone in your tree, minus the specific group of individuals you just filtered out.

11. Click **OK**. The Export window reopens. Before you continue, make sure the list contains every individual you want to include in your tree; you won't be able to restore any individuals once you've deleted them.

12. In **Output format,** choose "Family Tree Maker" and choose any other options as necessary. If you want your exported file to contain exactly the same information as your current tree, make sure to mark the Include private facts, notes, and media file options.

13. Click **OK**. The Export To window opens.

14. In the **Save in** field, choose the location where the exported file will be saved.

Family Tree Maker automatically names the exported file with the same name as the current tree. If you want to use a different name, you can change it in the File name field.

15. Click **Save**. A message tells you when your file has been exported successfully.

Detaching a Group of People in Your Tree

1. Go to the **Family** tab on the **People** workspace.

2. In the pedigree view or index click the name of the individual who is the root of the family or group of people you want to detach from your tree.

3. Click **Person**>**Attach/Detach Person**>**Detach Selected Person**. The Detach window opens. You will now choose which family the individual (and his ancestors) will be detached from (the individual's spouse and descendants or the individual's ancestors).

Detach Benjamin Hoyt ☒

Select the family from which you want to detach Benjamin Hoyt

○ **Existing family**

Father: John Hait (Hoyt)

Mother: Abigail Hait

Children: Samuel (Hoyt), William (Hoyt), John (Hoyt), Abigail (Hoyt), Benjamin Hoyt, Melancthon (Hoyt), Elizabeth (Hoyt), Mary (Hoyt), Joseph Warren (Hoyt), Gloriana (Hoyt), Leander (Hoyt)

○ **Existing family**

Father: Benjamin Hoyt

Mother: Elizabeth Reed

Children: Elizabeth Hoyt, Benjamin Hoyt, Emeline Hoyt, Julia Hoyt, James Hoyt, Eleanor Hoyt, Sarah Hoyt, Seymour Hoyt

[OK] [Cancel] [Help]

---

4. Choose the family from which you want to detach the individual.

5. Click **OK**. This branch of your family remains in your tree but is no longer connected to anyone. To access any of these individuals at a later time, you'll need to access them in the Index on the People workspace in order to view them in the pedigree view.

Attaching a Group of People to Your Tree

If you have a family that you discover is linked to your tree or you accidentally detach a group of people, you can quickly attach them to your tree as a group.

1. Go to the **Family** tab on the **People** workspace.

2. In the pedigree view or index click the name of the individual who is the root of the family or group of people you want to attach to your tree.

You can choose whether to attach the person to a father, mother, spouse, or child in your tree. In this case we'll attach the individual and their family to a father.

3. Click **Person>Attach/Detach Person>Attach Father**. The Select the Father to Attach window opens.

Name	Birth Date	Marr. Date	Death Date
Clason, Elizabeth			
Hait, Abigail	09 Oct 1740	31 Dec 1761	27 Feb 1796
Hait, Benjamin	02 Feb 1644	05 Jan 1670	26 Jan 1735
Hait, Benjamin	09 Dec 1671	10 Jun 1697	1747
Hait, Benjamin			
Hait, Deodate	13 Sep 1738		01 Mar 1796
Hait, Ebenezer	Oct 1712		Aug 1785
Hait, Hannah	17 Nov 1749		
Hait, Hannah	03 Jun 1676		
Hait, James	17 Feb 1742/43		14 Jul 1775
Hait, Mary	20 Sep 1673		
Hait, Mercy			Abt. 14 May 1...
Hait, Mercy	01 Jul 1746		16 Feb 1800
Hait, Neazer	08 Nov 1751		
Hait, Samuel	Bet. 1709-1718	Bet. 08 Mar 1...	06 Apr 1756
Hait, Samuel	Bet. 1679-1684		1766
Hait, Susanna	18 Sep 1754		02 Aug 1829
Hait, William	25 Apr 1743		15 Nov 1771
Hannah			

Find:

People: 59   OK   Cancel   Help

4. Choose the father's name from the list and click **OK**. The Attach Father window opens.

Attach father ☒

Select the family to which you want to attach Benjamin Hait as a father

Existing family
○ Father: Benjamin Hait
Mother: Hannah Weed
Children: Mary Hait, Hannah Hait, Samuel Hait

New Family
⊙ Father: Benjamin Hait
Mother: No mother entered
Children: Benjamin Hait

[OK] [Cancel] [Help]

5. Choose which father (and family) the individual will be attached to.

6. Click **OK**. The new branch of your family is now attached to your original tree.

Illegitimate Children

As you search for your family you may uncover some potentially painful and unnerving family facts—and one of the biggest can be illegitimate births. Even though I know the value of recording these types of facts and understand the importance of portraying an accurate picture of my ancestors' lives, I too felt reluctant to enter the facts about an illegitimate birth that occurred in my family.

If your family tree is for your personal use only, you can record illegitimate births in any way that makes sense to you. However, if you plan on putting your tree online, printing charts, or sharing your trees with others, you will want to be careful in how you approach these facts. This section shows a variety of ways that you can enter information about a child born out of wedlock, depending on the details you have discovered.

Entering a Private Note About a Birth

You can easily put information about an illegitimate birth in a person note, either for the specific individual or the mother or father.

1. Go to the **Family** tab on the **People** workspace.

2. In the pedigree view or index click the name of the individual you want to add a note to.

3. Click the **Person** tab; then click the **Notes** tab at the bottom of the window.

4. Click the **Person note** button in the notes toolbar.

5. Enter the text you want to include for the individual.

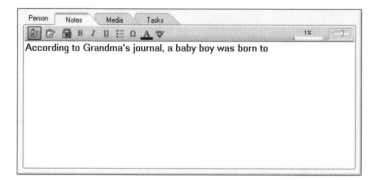

6. If you want to be able to exclude this note when you create reports or export your tree, click the **Mark as private** button in the notes toolbar.

> You can tell when a note has been marked as private because the lock button has a yellow box around it. To "unlock" the note, simply click the **Mark as private** button again.

Adding the Individual to Your Tree

In my tree, I chose to add the individual to my tree instead of entering a note about the birth. That way, I can enter facts about him, source my information, and keep track of what research I still need to do.

The way in which you'll add an individual depends on the data you've been able to gather and how the individual fits in your tree.

This task shows you how to add the individual if you have already entered the individual's father or mother in your tree; you may need to adapt these steps to your family's specific circumstances.

1. Go to the **Family** tab on the **People** workspace.

2. Click the name of the father or mother of the individual. In order to connect the child to a specific individual rather than a family that's already in place, it's easiest to use the Add Child menu option.

3. Click **Person>Add Person>Add Child**. The Add Child window opens.

4. Enter the child's name.

5. Choose a gender from the drop-down list and click **OK**. The individual's information is now displayed in the editing panel. You can enter any details, such as birth and death dates, that you have for the individual.

> When you enter a child's name, Family Tree Maker assumes that the child has the same surname as the father and adds his surname automatically. If the individual you're entering appears in records with another surname, you may want to enter the "correct" surname.

6. If you want to enter information about the individual's other parent, click **Add Mother** or **Add Father** from the **Person** menu and enter his or her information.

Choosing a Relationship Type for the Parents

When you enter parents for a child, Family Tree Maker automatically classifies the couple's relationship as "Spouses." In the case of illegitimate births, it is particularly important to clarify the type of relationship the two parents actually had.

1. Go to the **Family** tab on the **People** workspace.

2. In the pedigree view or index click the name of the father or mother of the individual.

3. Click the **Person** tab; then click the **Relationships** button.

4. Click the other parent's name under the "Spouse" heading.

5. In the editing panel, choose "Partner," "Other," or whatever is appropriate from the **Relationship** drop-down list.

Locations Report and Map

When you're tracking down records or trying to get a clear picture of all the locations where your ancestor lived, it can be helpful to create a report that lists every place you've entered for an individual. If you'd rather see a map of an individual's locations, you can do this too.

Creating a Locations Report for an Individual

1. Open the **Place Usage Report** (located on the Publish workspace under Place Reports).

2. Click the **Reset** button in the reports toolbar to clear any previous report settings.

3. Click **Individuals to Include**. The Filter Individuals window opens. Click the name of the person you want to create the report for and click **Include**.

Filter Individuals				
Name:				

Name	Birth		Name	Birth
[Hoyt], John Hait	24 Nov 1740	Include >		
[Shanklin], Permelia A.	Abt. 1814	Include All >>		
Adams, James		Ancestors >		
Bell, Abigail				
Bennington, Sarah	Abt. 1812	Descendants >		
Bobbitt, Alta M.	09 Feb 1892			
Bobbitt, Arthur L.	24 Aug 1897	Filter In... >		
Bobbitt, Bessie A.	14 Dec 1888			
Bobbitt, Charity M.	10 Mar 1883			
Bobbitt, Cornelia	Abt. 1856			
Bobbitt, Eugene A.	Jan 1877	< Exclude		
Bobbitt, Fern Edna	Apr 1909	<< Exclude All		
Bobbitt, Francis M.	Abt. 1869			
Bobbitt, Isham		< Filter Out...		
Bobbitt, James Clarence	28 Jul 1858			
Bobbitt, James Leslie	19 Sep 1884			
Bobbitt, Jessie	Abt. 1873			
Bobbitt, John W	Jun 1832			

Individuals included in list: 271 · · · · · · · · · Individuals included in filter: 0

[OK] [Cancel] [Help]

4. Click **OK**. The report will show every location associated with an individual, including facts and dates.

Place Usage Report Preview

81%

Place Usage Report for Julia Hoyt

Chillicothe, Ross, Ohio, USA
Hoyt, Julia
    Birth: 06 Sep 1834
Cortez, Montezuma, Colorado, USA
Hoyt, Julia
    Death: 23 Jul 1923
Dawson, Nebraska, USA
Hoyt, Julia
    Burial: 1923
Liberty, Richardson, Nebraska, USA
Hoyt, Julia
    Res: 1885
Roberts, Marshall, Illinois, USA
Hoyt, Julia
    Marr: 18 Oct 1852
    Res: 1860
    Res: 1870
Stapleton, Logan, Nebraska, USA
Hoyt, Julia
    Res: 1920
Van, Woods, Oklahoma
Hoyt, Julia
    Res: 1900

Page 1 of 1   Zoom Factor: 81%

Viewing a Map of an Individual's Locations

Family Tree Maker lets you see at a glance all the locations that are connected with a specific individual. You can even print these maps to take with you on research trips or to share with others.

1. Click the **Places** button on the main toolbar.

2. Choose "Person" from the **List by** drop-down list.

People: 252

List by: Person

Find: Place
          Person

3. Click the name of the individual whose locations you want to see. A road map will appear in the display area, and each location associated with an individual is indicated by a marker.

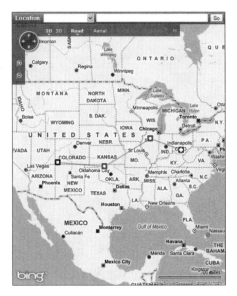

4. You can move the mouse over each marker to see the location's name and the fact associated with it.

5. To print the location map, click the **Print** button in the map toolbar and choose **Print Map** from the drop-down list. The Print window opens.

6. Choose a printer, select the number of copies to print, and click **OK**.

You can view the locations associated with an entire family by clicking the **Include immediate family** button in the Places toolbar.

Maiden Names

In genealogy, a woman is recorded using her maiden name, the surname she received at birth. Following this convention makes it easier to identify her parents. In addition, it is less likely people will misinterpret which family she belongs to. If you don't know a woman's maiden name, you can indicate this in a variety of ways; it doesn't really matter which method you choose, just be consistent. Somewhere in your tree you'll want to make a note of the conventions you are using.

Here are a few options you can use to indicate an unknown maiden name:

- Use square brackets and two hyphens (Margaret [--]).
- Use square brackets, a question mark, and hyphens (Margaret [--?--]).
- Enter "Unknown" (Margaret Unknown).
- Enter a question mark (Margaret ?).
- Enter the abbreviation MNU—Maiden Name Unknown (Margaret MNU). (Make sure you record the meaning of this abbreviation in your tree so others don't mistake it for a surname.)

You might also choose to leave out a maiden name entirely until you discover what it is.

Marriage

Almost nothing can tangle a family tree more quickly than a few unconventional marriages. When I look at my family tree, I see cousins who have married cousins, people with multiple marriages (some even to the same person), and even a polygamist or two. You might have a similar family history that includes step-brothers and step-sisters who marry, families with multiple sets of half-sisters and half-brothers, or an individual who marries multiple times.

Marriage Between Cousins

If your family history search takes you back very many years, you're bound to find at least one set of cousins in your tree who married each other. This wasn't unusual hundreds of years ago when people were born and lived in the same place their entire lives and marriage options were limited. You'll want to be careful when you enter these relationships in Family Tree Maker so you don't end up having the exact same family and duplicate individuals in two separate ancestral lines in your tree.

Follow these steps if only one individual is already in your tree:

1. Go to the **Family** tab on the **People** workspace.

2. In the pedigree view or index click the name of the individual.

3. Click **Add Spouse**.

4. Enter the name of the spouse (cousin), choose a gender, and click **OK**. The new spouse will become the focus of the pedigree view and family group view.

As you continue entering family names, the key to keeping your tree straight is to use the "attach" options on the Person menu. When you reach the point where the two cousins have a common ancestor, say if they have the same great-grandparents, you will enter the great-grandparents' names for one individual and then "attach" them to the other individual.

Follow these steps if both individuals (the cousins who married) are already in your tree but are not linked together:

1. Go to the **Family** tab on the **People** workspace.

2. In the pedigree view or index click the name of one of the individuals. Do not click "Add Spouse" to enter the spouse.

3. Choose **Person**>**Attach/Detach Person**>**Attach Spouse**. The Select the Spouse to Attach window opens.

Select The spouse To Attach			
Name	**Birth Date**	**Marr. Date**	**Death Date**
Hait, Benjamin	09 Dec 1671	10 Jun 1697	1747
Hait, Benjamin			
Hait, Deodate	13 Sep 1738		01 Mar 1796
Hait, Ebenezer	Oct 1712		Aug 1785
Hait, Ebenezer M.	Abt. 1710		
Hait, Hannah	17 Nov 1749		
Hait, Hannah	03 Jun 1676		
Hait, James	17 Feb 1742/43		14 Jul 1775
Hait, Mary	20 Sep 1673		
Hait, Mercy			Abt. 14 May 1...
Hait, Mercy	01 Jul 1746		16 Feb 1800
Hait, Mercy			
Hait, Neazer	08 Nov 1751		
Hait, Samuel	Bet. 1709-1718	Bet. 08 Mar 1...	06 Apr 1756
Hait, Samuel	Bet. 1679-1684		1766
Hait, Susanna	18 Sep 1754		02 Aug 1829
Hait, William	25 Apr 1743		15 Nov 1771
Hait, William			
Hannah			

People: 64   OK   Cancel   Help

4. Choose the spouse's name from the list and click **OK**. The Attach Spouse window opens.

5. Choose which family the spouse will be attached to (an existing family with children or a new family).

6. Click **OK**. The cousins are now shown as a couple in the pedigree view and family group view. Notice when you switch back and forth between the two spouses' names in the pedigree view, the names of the parents change, but the grandparents stay the same.

If you have entered duplicate family lines in your tree (for example, cousins married and you have entered the same family line twice), there is no easy fix to join the two branches together. The best work-around is to merge the duplicate individuals. Family Tree Maker contains a tool that can help you determine which individuals are duplicates. Follow these steps to find (and merge) duplicate family lines:

Before using the merge feature, you should back up your file because you cannot undo these changes.

1. Click **Edit>Find Duplicate People**. The Find Duplicate People window opens.

   In the first two columns you'll see the individuals who might be duplicates. Click a column header to sort the list alphabetically. In the third column you'll see a match score—the higher the number the more likely the individuals are a match; a 1,000 means the individuals are almost exact matches.

   Find Duplicate People ☐ □ ✕

Person 1	Person 2	Match Score
Hait, Mercy ()	Hait, Mercy (- 1787)	1000
Hait, Abigail (1740 -)	Hait, Abigail (1740 - 1796)	811
Hait, William ()	Hait, Neazer (1751 -)	684
Hait, Ebenezer M. (1710 -)	Hait, Ebenezer (1712 - 1785)	484
Hait, Benjamin ()	Hait, Benjamin (1644 - 1735)	427

   Total Matches: 5   [Go To Person]   [Remove Row]   [Compare/Merge...]   [Close]   [Help]

2. If you want to merge a pair of individuals (or just compare the two), click their row in the window and click **Compare/Merge**. The Individual Merge window opens.

3. In the Person 1 and Person 2 columns, choose how you want the individuals to be merged:

   - **Make preferred.** Enter the information as the "preferred" fact for the individual.
   - **Make alternate.** Enter the information as an alternate fact for the individual.

- **Discard this fact.** Do not merge the information into your tree. Click the **Keep sources** checkbox to merge the source information for the discarded fact.

The Merged Result column shows how the information will be merged together.

4. Click **OK** to complete the merge.

5. Repeat steps 2 through 4 for each duplicate individual in your tree.

Marriage to the Same Person Multiple Times

One of my uncles—I won't mention any names here—married and divorced the same woman twice, in addition to marrying two other times. Sometimes it's difficult to choose which wife is the "preferred" wife and document the duplicate marriages without making it seem like you've made a mistake. And it's even more complicated if children are involved. Fortunately, Family Tree Maker makes it fairly simple to record multiple marriages that involve the same individuals. This task assumes that you've already entered a previous marriage for the individuals.

1. Go to the **Family** tab on the **People** workspace.

2. In the pedigree view or index click the name of one of the individuals.

3. Click the **Person** tab; then click the **Facts** button. The Individual and Shared Facts workspace opens. You should be able to see the name of the spouse the selected individual has married multiple times.

4. Click the **Add Fact** (**+**) button in the toolbar. The Add Fact window opens.

5. In the Add Fact window, choose "Marriage" and click **OK**.

Facts	Type	
First Communion	Individual	OK
Funeral	Individual	Cancel
Graduation	Individual	
Height	Individual	Help
Immigration	Individual	
Marriage	Shared	
Marriage Bann	Shared	New...
Marriage Contract	Shared	
Marriage License	Shared	
Marriage Settlement	Shared	
Medical Condition	Individual	
Military Serial Number	Individual	
Military Service	Individual	
Mission (LDS)	Individual	
Name	Individual	
Namesake	Individual	
Nationality	Individual	

6. In the editing panel, enter the marriage's date and location. Then choose the name of the spouse in the drop-down list.

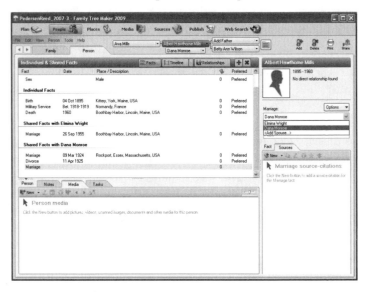

Both marriages now appear on the Individual and Shared Facts workspace.

Shared Facts with Dana Monroe				
Marriage	09 Mar 1924	Rockport, Essex, Massachusetts, USA	0	
Divorce	11 Apr 1925		0	Preferred
Marriage	01 Jan 1930	Boston, Middlesex, Massachusetts, USA	0	Preferred

Multiple Spouses

You may need to add more than one spouse for an individual—for example, if a widower or divorcée remarries. After you've entered both spouses, you'll need to choose a "preferred" spouse. Usually this is the spouse whose children are in your direct line. This preferred spouse will be the default spouse displayed in the family group view, pedigree view, and charts and reports.

1. Go to the **Family** tab on the **People** workspace.

2. In the pedigree view or index click the name of the individual you want to add a second spouse to.

3. In the family group view, click the **Spouse** icon next to the individual for whom you want to add an additional spouse. From the drop-down list, you have the choice of accessing the information for an existing spouse or adding a new spouse.

4. Choose **Add Spouse** from the drop-down list. The Add Spouse window opens.

5. Enter the spouse's name in the blank field and click **OK**. Family Tree Maker displays a new family group view, including the new spouse.

You'll now need to choose which is the "preferred" spouse.

6. Make sure the individual with multiple spouses is the focus of the pedigree view and the family group view on the Family tab.

7. Click the **Person** tab; then click the **Relationships** button. You should see two names listed under the "Spouses" heading.

8. In the **Spouses** list, click the name of the individual whom you want to become the preferred spouse.

9. In the editing panel, click the **Preferred spouse** checkbox.

If information about a spouse isn't appearing on the Person tab in the Facts section or Timeline, it could be that you haven't entered a marriage date for the couple. If you don't know the exact marriage date, you can still enter an estimated date, use date ranges, or use "Bef." (Before) or "Aft." (After).

Maternal Ancestors Report

You can create a report that includes only your maternal ancestors (your mother and her direct ancestors). This can be helpful when you are focusing on this side of your family tree.

1. Open the **Custom Report** (located on the Publish workspace under Person Reports).

2. Click the **Reset** button in the reports toolbar to clear any previous report settings.

3. In **Individuals to include**, click **Selected individuals**. The Filter Individuals window opens. No individuals should be included in the report at this point; if there are, click **Exclude All** to clear the report.

4. Click your mother's name in the **Name** list and click **Ancestors**.

5. Choose your report options and click **OK**. You can choose the number of generations included and whether to include all parents and spouses. In this case, I want only direct-line ancestors, so I'll include only preferred spouses and parents.

The list will include all your maternal ancestors—male and female.

6. Click **OK**. The report opens.

Men-Only Report

If you want to focus on finding information about only your male relatives, it can be helpful to create a report that lists only the men in your family tree.

1. Open the **Custom Report** (located on the Publish workspace under Person Reports).

2. Click the **Reset** button in the reports toolbar to clear any previous report settings.

3. In **Individuals to include**, click **Selected individuals**. The Filter Individuals window opens. No individuals should be included in the report at this point; if there are, click **Exclude All** to clear the report.

4. Click **Filter In**. The Filter Individuals by Criteria window opens.

5. Click **Vital facts**.

6. Choose "Sex" from the **Search where** drop-down list.

7. Choose "Equals" from the next drop-down list.

8. Choose "Male" from the **Value** drop-down list.

9. Click **OK**. The Filter Individuals window now shows all the males in your family tree. You can filter the list further if necessary.

10. Click **OK**. The report opens.

Military Service Report

A family member's military service leaves a trail of records full of important information—you may have pension and service records or even draft cards. If you have included military facts for individuals in your tree, you can create a report of this information.

Adding Military Information for an Individual

Before you can generate a military service report, you need to enter any pertinent military facts in your tree.

1. Go to the **Family** tab on the **People** workspace.

2. In the pedigree view or index click the name of the individual for whom you want to add military information.

3. Click the **Person** tab; then click the **Facts** button. The Individual and Shared Facts workspace opens.

4. Click the **Add Fact** (+) button in the toolbar. The Add Fact window opens.

Facts	Type
Height	Individual
Immigration	Individual
Marriage	Shared
Marriage Bann	Shared
Marriage Contract	Shared
Marriage License	Shared
Marriage Settlement	Shared
Medical Condition	Individual
Military Serial Number	Individual
Military Service	Individual
Mission (LDS)	Individual
Name	Individual
Namesake	Individual
Nationality	Individual
Naturalization	Individual
Occupation	Individual
Ordination	Individual

Buttons: OK, Cancel, Help, New...

5. Click "Military Service" in the **Facts** list and click **OK**. If you've created other custom military facts, such as Civil War or Korean War, you can select this fact from the Facts list.

6. In the individual's editing panel, enter the military information in the date, place, and description fields.

Creating a Military Service Report

1. Open the **Custom Report** (located on the Publish workspace under Person Reports).

2. Click the **Reset** button in the reports toolbar to clear any previous report settings.

3. Click the **Items to include** button in the reports toolbar. The Items to Include window opens.

Because you're creating a report about military service, you'll need to add this fact to the report.

4. Click the blue button. The Select Fact window opens.

5. Choose "Military Service" from the **Facts** list.

6. Click **OK**. If you have additional custom military facts, such as Civil War, Korean War, or Military Pension, you might want to repeat steps 4 through 6 to add these facts too.

You can now delete any facts you don't want to include in the report.

7. In the **Included facts** list, highlight a fact, such as birth, and click the red button.

8. Click **OK**. The report is displayed. If you want the report to display only individuals in your tree who have military facts recorded, continue with the following steps:

9. In **Individuals to include**, click **Selected individuals**. The Filter Individuals window opens. No individuals should be included in the report at this point; if there are, click **Exclude All** to clear the report.

10. Click **Filter In**. The Filter Individuals by Criteria window opens.

11. Click **All facts**.

12. Choose "Military Service" from the **Search where** drop-down list; then choose "Date" or "Place."

13. Choose "Is not blank" from the next drop-down list.

14. Click **OK**. The Filter Individuals window now shows all the individuals for whom you have recorded information in the Military Service fact. Repeat steps 10 through 14 for each custom military fact you've created until all the individuals whose facts you want included are in the list.

15. Click **OK** on the Filter Individuals window. The report opens.

Missing Date Reports

When I first started my family tree it was fairly easy to keep track of which facts I'd found and see gaping holes where I was missing information. But the deeper I went to explore my roots, the more I had a tendency to get sidetracked. The Illinois state censuses just came online? I better go look; right now. And when I found a photo of a tombstone (that no one knew existed) for my grandma's twin on Findagrave.com, you can bet I spent a few days completely ignoring my current research as I hunted through the rest of the website.

If your unexpected finds take you down a different path than the one you were on, you may not realize the blanks you have left in your family tree. Periodically I will run a few custom reports to find out what information I've neglected. The missing dates I look for most often are for births, deaths, and marriages, but you can modify these reports to look for the missing dates for any fact.

I recommend creating a separate report for each fact. Otherwise, it's harder to determine what dates are missing for each individual—he or she may be missing all dates or just one.

Creating a Missing Birth Date Report

1. Open the **Custom Report** (located on the Publish workspace under Person Reports).

2. Click the **Reset** button in the reports toolbar to clear any previous report settings.

3. Click the **Items to include** button in the reports toolbar. The Items to Include window opens.

You'll now delete the marriage and death facts that are included automatically in the report.

4. In the **Included facts** list, highlight "Marriage" and click the red button. Repeat this step for the "Death" fact.

5. Click **OK**. The report opens again.

6. In **Individuals to include**, click **Selected individuals**. The Filter Individuals window opens. No individuals should be included in the report at this point; if there are, click **Exclude All** to clear the report.

7. Click **Filter In**. The Filter Individuals by Criteria window opens.

8. Click **Vital facts**.

9. Choose "Birth" from the **Search where** drop-down list; then choose "Date."

10. Choose "Is blank" from the next drop-down list.

11. Click **OK**. The Filter Individuals window now shows all the individuals who do not have birth dates recorded in your tree.

12. Click **OK** on the Filter Individuals window. The report opens.

Creating a Missing Marriage Date Report

1. Open the **Custom Report** (located on the Publish workspace under Person Reports).

2. Click the **Reset** button in the reports toolbar to clear any previous report settings.

3. Click the **Items to include** button in the reports toolbar. The Items to Include window opens.

You'll now delete the birth and death facts that are included automatically in the report.

4. In the **Included facts** list, highlight "Birth" and click the red button. Repeat this step for the "Death" fact.

5. Click **OK**. The report opens again.

6. In **Individuals to include**, click **Selected individuals**. The Filter Individuals window opens. No individuals should be included in the report at this point; if there are, click **Exclude All** to clear the report.

7. Click **Filter In**. The Filter Individuals by Criteria window opens.

8. Click **Vital facts**.

9. Choose "Marriage" from the **Search where** drop-down list; then choose "Date."

10. Choose "Is blank" from the next drop-down list.

11. Click **OK**. The Filter Individuals window now shows all the individuals who do not have marriage dates recorded in your tree.

12. Click **OK** on the Filter Individuals window. The report opens.

Creating a Missing Death Date Report

1. Open the **Custom Report** (located on the Publish workspace under Person Reports).

2. Click the **Reset** button in the reports toolbar to clear any previous report settings.

3. Click the **Items to include** button in the reports toolbar. The Items to Include window opens.

You'll now delete the birth and marriage facts that are included automatically in the report.

4. In the **Included facts** list, highlight "Birth" and click the red (X) button. Repeat this step for the "Marriage" fact.

5. Click **OK**. The report opens again.

6. In **Individuals to include**, click **Selected individuals**. The Filter Individuals window opens. No individuals should be included in the report at this point; if there are, click **Exclude All** to clear the report.

7. Click **Filter In**. The Filter Individuals by Criteria window opens.

8. Click **Vital facts**.

9. Choose "Death" from the **Search where** drop-down list; then choose "Date."

10. Choose "Is blank" from the next drop-down list.

11. Click **OK**. The Filter Individuals window now shows all the individuals who do not have death dates recorded in your tree.

12. Click **OK** on the Filter Individuals window. The report opens.

Creating a Missing Dates Report for Direct Ancestors

The three previous reports will show the missing dates for every individual included in your family tree. If you want, you can create the same reports for only your direct ancestors.

1. Open the **Custom Report** (located on the Publish workspace under Person Reports).

2. Click the **Reset** button in the reports toolbar to clear any previous report settings.

3. Click the **Items to include** button in the reports toolbar. The Items to Include window opens.

4. Delete the facts you don't want included in the report. In this example, I'll keep the birth fact.

5. Click **OK**. The report opens again.

6. In **Individuals to include**, click **Selected individuals**. The Filter Individuals window opens. No individuals should be included in the report at this point; if there are, click **Exclude All** to clear the report.

7. Click your name in the **Name** list and click **Ancestors**.

8. Choose your report options and click **OK**. You can choose the number of generations included and whether to include all parents and spouses. In this case, I want only direct-line ancestors so I'll include only preferred spouses and parents.

Now you can filter out the individuals who don't have missing dates—in this example, missing birth dates.

9. In the Filter Individuals window click **Filter Out**. The Filter Individuals by Criteria window opens.

10. Click **Vital facts**.

11. Choose "Birth" from the **Search where** drop-down list; then choose "Date."

12. Because we already have a group of people and are excluding individuals, you'll choose "Is not blank" from the next drop-down list.

13. Click **OK**. The Filter Individuals window now shows all your direct ancestors who do not have birth dates recorded in your tree.

14. Click **OK** on the Filter Individuals window. The report opens.

Custom Report Preview

81%

Missing Birth Dates
Direct Ancestors Only

David Hitchcock		
George Thompson		
Isham Bobbitt		
Margaret Smith		
Mary Rush		
	Birth:	England
Morten Pedersen		
	Birth:	Gunderup, Denmark
Peder Christian Anderson		
	Birth:	Denmark
Robb Bush		
	Birth:	England
Robert Smith		
Sarah Thompson		
	Birth:	England
Thomas Gold		
William Bennington Sr		

Page 1 of 1

Zoom Factor: 81%

Moving Files Between Computers

When you purchase a new computer system, it's always a little nerve-wracking trying to make sure that all your files from your old computer make it onto the new one. This task will help you get your Family Tree Maker software and files up and running in no time.

1. Install your most current version of Family Tree Maker on your new computer. (When you place the installation CD in the CD drive the installation should begin immediately.)

2. On your old computer, you will need to create a backup file of the Family Tree Maker tree that you want to transfer to the new computer. Make sure the tree you want to back up is open; then click **File>Backup**. The Backup window opens.

3. If you want a new name to distinguish this backup file from your original tree, enter a new name for the tree in the **Backup file name** field. For example, a name like "PedersenTree_NEW."

You can now choose whether to back up your file to a floppy disk, CD, DVD, or flash drive.

4. Insert your CD or DVD in your disk drive or connect your flash drive to your old computer.

5. In "Backup location," click **Removeable Media** and choose your CD-ROM drive, DVD drive, or flash drive from the drop-down list.

6. Click the **Include linked media files** checkbox. If you don't, photos, videos, and audio items you've linked to your tree in Family Tree Maker won't be included in the backup file.

7. Click **OK**. A series of messages shows the progress of the backup.

8. When the backup is complete, take your CD, DVD, or flash drive and insert it in your new computer.

   Now you need to copy the backup file to your new computer's hard drive.

9. On the new computer, double-click **My Computer** and browse to the drive where your backup file is stored (CD, DVD, or flash drive).

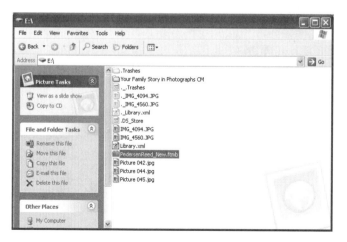

10. Once you have found your backup (.ftmb) file, right-click it and select **Copy**.

11. Find the folder on your hard drive where you want to store the file (such as My Documents); then right-click and select **Paste**. The backup file is now copied to your hard drive.

12. Open Family Tree Maker on your new computer.

13. Choose **File>Restore**. The Choose File to Restore window opens.

14. Click the **Look in** drop-down list and find the folder where the backup (.ftmb) file is located.

15. Click the backup file you want to open.

16. Click **Open**. The Name for Restored File window opens.

You'll now create a new Family Tree Maker tree from your backup file.

17. In the **Save in** field, choose a location for the new file.

18. In the **File name** field, enter a name for the new file.

19. Click **Save**. Your tree opens in Family Tree Maker. Notice that your media items are saved in the same folder where you just saved your new tree.

You'll now have two Family Tree Maker files on your new computer—a regular Family Tree Maker file (.ftm) and a backup file (.ftmb). You can delete the backup file or keep it in case you need to restore your tree again.

Moving Files Between Computers

Name Suffixes

Name suffixes such as Jr. (Junior), Sr. (Senior), and III (the Third) can be helpful in distinguishing between ancestors with the same or similar names. When you enter a name suffix, you do not need to place a comma between the individual's surname and his or her name suffix (for example, John Bobbitt, Sr.). Family Tree Maker recognizes these as name suffixes and sorts them correctly in reports and charts.

1. Go to the **Family** tab on the **People** workspace.

2. In the pedigree view or index, click on an individual's name.

3. In the editing panel, enter the individual's name in the **Name** field. After the surname, enter the appropriate abbreviation (for example, enter "Tyler Reed Jr.").

> Do not enter name suffixes in the Title field. This field is reserved for honorary titles such as Lady, Reverend, or Doctor.

Nicknames

Growing up, I had always known one of my great-aunts as Tally. An unusual name? Yes, but she was older. Who knew what people named their children at the turn of the century, right? I naturally assumed that was her name—until I started searching for my family's history. One quick call to my parents and I discovered her given name was actually Sarah Jane. Without this information I would have been stumped and unable to figure out why I couldn't find any records for her. Crisis averted.

If one of your family members was known by a nickname rather than his or her given name, you'll want to enter this in your Family Tree Maker tree. If the nickname is a common one (for example, Tim for Timothy), this might not be necessary. But, if the nickname is unconventional or uncommon, as it was with my great-aunt, you'll want to record this.

You can indicate a nickname by using quotation marks (for example, Sarah Jane "Tally" Gedge). Or, you can use the Also Known As fact to record a nickname.

Paternal Ancestors Report

You can create a report that includes only your paternal ancestors (your father and his direct ancestors). This can be helpful when you are focusing on this side of your family tree.

1. Open the **Custom Report** (located on the Publish workspace under Person Reports).

2. Click the **Reset** button in the reports toolbar to clear any previous report settings.

3. In **Individuals to include**, click **Selected individuals**. The Filter Individuals window opens. No individuals should be included in the report at this point; if there are, click **Exclude All** to clear the report.

4. Click your father's name in the **Name** list.

5. Click **Ancestors**. The list will include all your paternal ancestors—male and female.

6. Click **OK**. The report opens.

Custom Report Preview

81% ▾ ⊖ ⊕ ◁ ▷ ▷| ⊞

Paternal Ancestors Report

Cyrus Henry Gold
Birth: 01 May 1848 in Birmingham, Warwick, England
Marriage: Abt. 1871
Marriage: 08 Aug 1904 in Salt Lake City, Salt Lake, Utah, USA
Death: 27 Mar 1930 in Salt Lake City, Salt Lake, Utah

Elray Lincoln Pedersen
Birth: 12 Feb 1937 in Salt Lake City, Utah, USA
Marriage: 21 Dec 1962 in Salt Lake City, UT, USA

George Thompson

Herbert Bush Gedge
Birth: 10 Nov 1872 in Salt Lake City, Salt Lake, Utah, USA
Marriage: 20 Nov 1895 in Salt Lake City, Salt Lake, Utah, USA
Death: 09 Aug 1942 in Salt Lake City, Salt Lake, Utah, USA

Joseph Gold
Birth: England
Marriage: 27 Jan 1845 in Warwick, England
Marriage: 20 Jun 1861 in Aston, Warwickshire, England

Louise Fannie Newman
Birth: Abt. 1865 in England

M. K. Petersen
Birth: Denmark

Mary Rush
Birth: England

Mary Willis
Birth: 05 Sep 1852 in Kineton, Warwickshire, England

Page 1 of 2   Zoom Factor: 81%

Same-Sex Relationships

Family Tree Maker is flexible enough to show different types of non-traditional relationships. If you have a couple in your tree who are in a same-sex relationship, you can indicate this in your tree.

1. Go to the **Family** tab on the **People** workspace.

2. Enter the first individual's information into your tree.

3. In the family group view, click **Add Spouse**.

4. Enter the second individual's name, choose a gender from the drop-down list, and click **OK**.

5. Click the **Person** tab for either individual; then click the **Relationships** button.

6. Under the **Spouse** heading, choose the individual's name.

7. In the editing panel, choose the correct relationship type from the **Relationship** drop-down list (for example, friend or partner). You can also choose a status for the relationship from the **Status** drop-down list.

Surnames

Multi-Word Surnames

In some instances, a surname (last name) is made up of multiple words, such as "de Beaumont." In other cases, an individual may have two surnames, such as Pérez Mártinez—one inherited from his father and one from his mother. Because Family Tree Maker automatically assumes that the last word in the Name fact is the individual's surname, multi-word surnames will be alphabetized and indexed incorrectly unless you identify them in the software. To indicate a multi-word surname, you can use backward slashes (\). For example, in the Name fact, you would enter "Peter \Van der Voort\" or "Diana \St. John\".

Duplicate Surnames

Occasionally, you may find a female ancestor whose last name at birth is the same as her husband's surname; in other words, her maiden name and her married name are the same. This happened quite often in certain areas such as Scandinavia, where patronymics were used for centuries. In my family, my Danish great-grandparents were both born Pedersens. To someone unfamiliar with my family tree, this name du-

Patronymics is a naming system where a child's surname is derived from his or her father's name—the name of the father plus a suffix or prefix. For example, the son of Soren could have the surname Sorensen or the daughter of Willem could have the surname Willemsdockter.

plication might appear to be a mistake. To prevent any confusion, I have entered a personal note that explains why both surnames are the same.

Hyphenated Surnames

In recent decades, many women have forgone traditional name changes when they marry. Some women keep their maiden name and some choose to hyphenate their maiden name with their husband's surname. Although a woman is recorded in a tree with the name she received when she was born, you'll want to record any legal name changes, such as added hyphens.

1. Go to the People workspace and click the **Person** tab for the individual you want to add information for.

2. Click the **Facts** button. The Individual and Shared Facts workspace opens.

3. Click the **Add Fact** (+) button in the toolbar. The Add Fact window opens.

4. Click "Also Known As" in the **Facts** list and click **OK**.

5. In the individual's editing panel, enter any dates associated with the name change in the **Date** field (the default field); in the **Description** field, enter the alternate name. Don't forget to add source information for the name change.

Surname Variations

Peterson, Pettersen, or Pedersen? In my extended family, different branches of my father's family have chosen to spell our last name in a variety of ways. Over the years, the spelling of your surname may have changed too. In some cases this happens when a family immigrates to a new country and changes their name so it is easier to pronounce or spell. For others, names have been recorded phonetically—which can mean the surname is spelled differently on every record. Regardless of the reason, you'll want to search for your family members under all these names and include the alternate spellings in your tree.

You may want to add the alternate surname as a note. Or you can follow this task and add the name in the Also Known As fact.

1. Go to the People workspace and click the **Person** tab for the individual you want to add information for.

2. Click the **Facts** button. The Individual and Shared Facts workspace opens.

3. Click the **Add Fact** (+) button in the toolbar. The Add Fact window opens.

4. Click "Also Known As" in the **Facts** list and click **OK**.

5. In the individual's editing panel, enter any dates associated with the name in the **Date** field (the default field); in the **Description** field, enter the alternate name. Don't forget to add source information for the name variation.

Creating a Surname Report

If you're researching one branch of your family tree it can be helpful to create a report of all individuals with the same surname.

1. Open the **Custom Report** (located on the Publish workspace under Person Reports).

2. Click the **Reset** button in the reports toolbar to clear any previous report settings.

3. In **Individuals to include**, click **Selected individuals**. The Filter Individuals window opens. No individuals should be included in the report at this point; if there are, click **Exclude All** to clear the report.

4. Click **Filter In**. The Filter Individuals by Criteria window opens.

5. Click **Vital facts**.

6. Choose "Name" from the **Search where** drop-down list.

7. Choose "Contains" from the next drop-down list.

8. In the **Value** field, enter a surname (for example, enter "Bobbitt").

9. Click **OK**. The Filter Individuals window now shows all the individuals who have the same surname. You can filter the list further if necessary.

10. Click **OK** on the Filter Individuals window. The report opens.

Custom Report Preview

81%

BOBBITTS

Alta M. Bobbitt
Birth: 09 Feb 1892 in Kansas
Death: 04 Nov 1987 in Cherokee, Alfalfa, Oklahoma

Arthur L. Bobbitt
Birth: 24 Aug 1897 in Oklahoma
Death: 05 Jun 1993 in Oklahoma City, Oklahoma, Oklahoma

Bessie A. Bobbitt
Birth: 14 Dec 1888 in Nebraska

Charity M. Bobbitt
Birth: 10 Mar 1883 in Nebraska
Death: May 1982 in Gering, Scotts Bluff, Nebraska

Cornelia Bobbitt
Birth: Abt. 1856 in Illinois

Eugene A. Bobbitt
Birth: Jan 1877 in Illinois

Fern Edna Bobbitt
Birth: Apr 1909 in Oklahoma
Death: 17 Aug 1997 in Las Cruces, Dona Ana, New Mexico, United States of America

Francis M. Bobbitt
Birth: Abt. 1869 in Illinois

Isham Bobbitt
Marriage: 21 Dec 1824 in Trigg, Kentucky

James Clarence Bobbitt
Birth: 28 Jul 1858 in Illinois

Page 1 of 2   Zoom Factor: 81%

Titles

Some of your family members may have titles such as Doctor, Reverend, or Colonel associated with them. These titles can be useful when trying to distinguish between ancestors with the same or similar names. In my maternal branch, I have five Samuel Haits—and that's just in my direct line. Luckily some of the records I've found include titles, so I can tell Captain Sam Hait from Deacon Samuel Hait. Family Tree Maker makes this easy to record in the Title fact.

1. Go to the People workspace and click the **Person** tab for the individual you want to add information for.

2. Click the **Facts** button. The Individual and Shared Facts workspace opens.

3. Click the **Add Fact** (+) button in the toolbar. The Add Fact window opens.

Facts	Type		
Phone Number	Individual		**OK**
Physical Description	Individual		**Cancel**
Probate	Individual		
Property	Individual		**Help**
Reference ID	Individual		
Reference ID	Shared		
Religion	Individual		**New...**
Residence	Individual		
Retirement	Individual		
Sealed to Parents (LDS)	Individual		
Sealed to Spouse (LDS)	Shared		
Separation	Shared		
Social Security Number	Individual		
Title	Individual		
Web Address	Individual		
Weight	Individual		
Will	Individual		

4. Click "Title" in the **Facts** list and click **OK**.

5. In the individual's editing panel, enter the title in the **Description** field. Then enter any dates associated with the title in the **Date** field. Don't forget to add source information.

Twins and Multiple Births

If you have a family member who is a twin, triplet, or part of a multiple birth, you'll want to indicate this in your Family Tree Maker tree. This information could lead to additional birth certificates or family facts that you might not find otherwise.

A 1910 census record for my maternal great-grandparents indicated that my great-grandmother had given birth to twelve children—nine of whom were living. I had information—and photos—for the nine children. But who were the missing ones? Luckily I knew that my grandmother had a twin who had died when she was only thirteen months old. That left only two unaccounted-for children. I soon found information about them on a family plaque that memorialized these two who had died young. If I hadn't known my grandmother had a twin who died young, I could have spent months or years looking for a child who wasn't really missing.

You can include this type of birth information in a personal note; or, if you want to be able to see this at a glance, you might want to include this information in the Name fact. Simply enter the name followed by a comma and the individual's birth information (for example, enter "Maurine Bobbitt, twin"). If you choose this last option, make sure you record this convention somewhere in your tree so people don't accidentally think that "twin" is a name suffix.

Unmarried Parents

Unmarried parents still need to be entered in Family Tree Maker as a "couple." But you can indicate that the two were never married and specify the type of relationship they had.

1. Go to the **Family** tab on the **People** workspace.

2. In the pedigree view or index click the name of the couple's child.

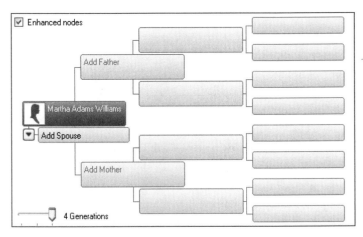

3. Click **Add Father** and **Add Mother** and add the individual's parents.

4. Click the **Person** tab; then click the **Relationships** button.

5. Click the individual's name under the **Spouse** heading.

6. In the editing panel, choose "Partner," "Friend," or whatever is appropriate from the **Relationship** drop-down list.

Unrelated Individuals

In your searches, you may come across an individual who might be related to you but you're unable to determine a connection. You don't want to connect this individual to anyone in your tree until you're certain they're family, but you don't want to lose his or her information in case you discover a relationship with the person at a later time. In these cases, you'll want to add the individual to your tree without linking them with anyone.

I found a death index entry for an infant that bore the fairly unique surname of my great-grandfather. I wasn't sure whether this was one of his children, but I added the individual to my tree "just in case." Months later when I was able to view the actual death certificate, I learned that this baby was indeed one of his children. Because I had already added this person to my tree, it was easy to simply link her to her parents.

1. Click the **People** button on the main toolbar.

2. Click **Person>Add Person>Add Unrelated Person**. The Add Unrelated Person window opens.

3. Enter the person's name (first name, middle name, and last name).

4. Choose a gender from the drop-down list and click **OK**. The new individual becomes the focus of the pedigree view and editing panel.

> Because the individual isn't connected to anyone else in your tree, you can navigate to him or her only by clicking his or her name in the index on the People workspace.

Visually-Impaired Users

If you've ever spent hours in front of a computer monitor, you've probably reached a point where you wish everything on your screen was just a little bit bigger. Whether you experience occasional eye strain or have real difficulty viewing your computer screen, here are a few tricks that might help.

Enlarging the Font in Family Tree Maker

1. Click **Tools**>**Options**.

2. Click the **General** tab.

3. Click the **Use large fonts** checkbox.

4. Click **OK**.

Changing Your Windows Settings

1. Right-click your computer desktop and select **Properties**. The Display Properties window opens.

2. Click the **Settings** tab.

3. In "Screen resolution" drag the slider bar to the left. The more you move toward "Less," the larger windows and text will appear on your monitor. A standard large-resolution choice is 800 by 600.

4. Click **OK**.

On the facing page you can see the difference between a desktop at 1280 by 1024 resolution and an enlarged desktop at 800 by 600 resolution.

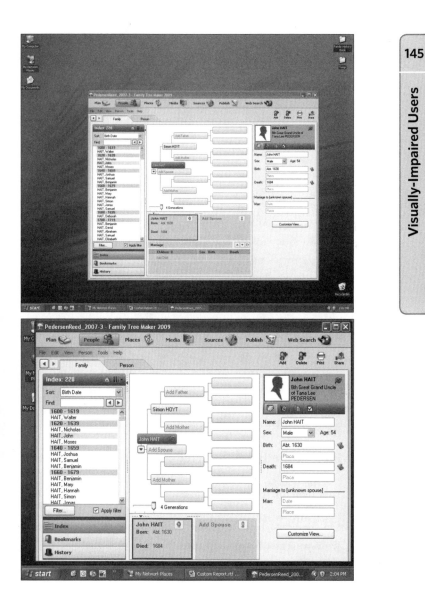

Web Clipping

You've probably used Family Tree Maker to merge facts and records from Ancestry.com into your tree. But did you know you can capture text and images from other websites and merge them into your tree too? It's called Web clipping, and it's one of my favorite tools.

When I was unable to find my grandfather's immigration records in Ancestry databases, I went looking on the Web for other resources. On the Danish State Archives website, I found emigration records for his entire family and used the Web clipping tool to quickly add the information to my tree. Later, I came across a photo of the ship they sailed on to America and was able to add it to my tree also.

If you find online information (such as a marriage date, family photograph, or town description) you want to add to your tree, you don't have to enter the information manually; let Family Tree Maker do the work for you.

> Before downloading text or images from the Web, make sure you aren't violating any copyright restrictions or get permission from the owner.

Saving Online Facts to a Tree

1. On the Web Search workspace, access the website you want to "clip" information from.

2. On the Facts tab at the bottom of the window, click the **Person from your tree** button and select the individual you want to link the information to.

3. On the Search Result Detail toolbar, click the **Enable Web clipping** button.

Enable Web clipping button

4. Highlight the text on the website. The Insert Fact drop-down list appears.

5. Choose a fact from the drop-down list. For example, you can choose the birthplace fact. The information now appears in the Search Result Detail section.

6. When you have selected all the information you want from the website, click the **Merge** button on the Search Result Detail toolbar. The Web Merge Wizard will launch.

Saving Online Images to a Tree

1. On the Web Search workspace, access the website you want to "clip" an image from.

2. On the Media tab at the bottom of the window, click the **Person from your tree** button and select the individual you want to link the information to.

3. On the Search Result Detail toolbar, click the **Enable Web clipping** button.

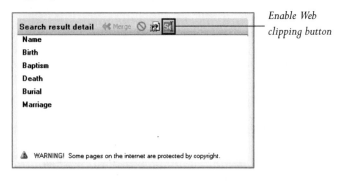

Enable Web clipping button

4. Move the cursor over the browser window until the image you want is highlighted by a green dotted line.

5. Click the highlighted image. A thumbnail of the image appears in the Search Result Detail section.

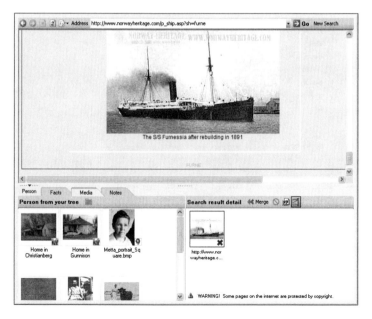

6. When you have selected all the photos you want from the web-site, click the **Merge** button on the Search Result Detail toolbar. The Web Merge Wizard will launch.

Saving Online Text to a Tree

1. On the Web Search workspace, access the website you want to "clip" information from.

2. On the Notes tab at the bottom of the window, click the **Person from your tree** button and select the individual you want to link the information to.

3. On the Search Result Detail toolbar, click the **Enable Web clip-ping** button (the button on the far right).

Enable Web clipping button

4. Highlight the text on the website.

5. Click the **Insert Note** button that appears.

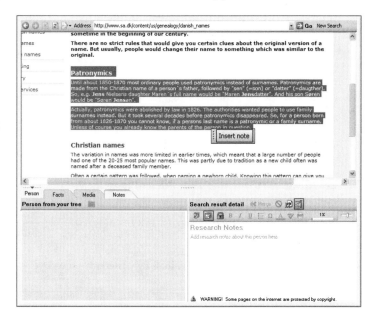

6. When you have selected all the text you want from the website, click the **Merge** button on the Search Result Detail toolbar. The Web Merge Wizard will launch.

Women-Only Report

If you want to focus on finding information about only your female relatives, it can be helpful to create a report that lists only the women in your family tree.

1. Open the **Custom Report** (located on the Publish workspace under Person Reports).

2. Click the **Reset** button in the reports toolbar to clear any previous report settings.

3. In **Individuals to include**, click **Selected individuals**. The Filter Individuals window opens. No individuals should be included in the report at this point; if there are, click **Exclude All** to clear the report.

4. Click **Filter In**. The Filter Individuals by Criteria window opens.

Filter Individuals By Criteria			☒
⊙ Vital facts	○ All facts	○ Other	
Search where:		Value:	
Sex ⌄	Equals ⌄	Female ⌄	
		OK Cancel Help	

5. Click **Vital facts**.

6. Choose "Sex" from the **Search where** drop-down list.

7. Choose "Equals" from the next drop-down list.

8. Choose "Female" from the **Value** drop-down list.

9. Click **OK**. The Filter Individuals window now shows all the females in your family tree. You can filter the list further if necessary.

10. Click **OK**. The report opens.

Index

About the Author

Tana L. Pedersen

Tana has been writing and editing in the technology industry for more than ten years. In that time, she has earned several awards for her writing, including the Distinguished Technical Communication award from the Society for Technical Communication. She is a contributing editor to *Ancestry* magazine, author of *The Official Guide to Family Tree Maker 2009, The Official Guide to Family Tree Maker 2010, The Family Tree Maker 2009 Little Book of Answers*, and co-author of *The Official Guide to RootsWeb.com*.

Photo by Braden Lord